Memorize in Minutes:

The TIMES TABLES

By Alan Walker

Illustrated by Jesus Murillo

Krimsten Publishing, Washington

Memorize in Minutes:

The TIMES TABLES

By Alan Walker

Published by:

Krimsten Publishing
Post Office Box 48
Prosser, Washington 99350-0048 U.S.A.

International Standard Book Number: 0-9651769-6-7

Library of Congress Catalog Card Number: 98-87549

Attention: Corporations and Schools
   Krimsten Publishing books are available at quantity discounts with bulk purchase for educational, business, or sales promotional use. For information, please write to: Krimsten Publishing Special Sales, P.O. Box 48, Prosser, WA 99350. Please supply: title of book, ISBN number, quantity, how the book will be used, and date needed.

Table of Contents

Contents

Introduction

The multiplication facts are building blocks for mathematics. A student who has not memorized the basic multiplication facts has difficulty succeeding in almost all areas of mathematics. Knowing the multiplication facts is a necessity for much of the math taught above the third grade.

Traditionally, students have been told to 'memorize' the basic facts, yet they are not taught how to memorize. For years, teachers have relied on rote memory. Rote memory, or repeating the facts over and over again, has been shown to be the **least** effective method of memorizing. Memorize in Minutes: The Times Tables uses mnemonic devices to help students remember. A mnemonic device is a technique used to assist memory.

Memorize in Minutes

Numbers and number combinations comprise the most difficult information to remember. Numbers are abstract, not concrete or tangible. It is extremely difficult for the brain to file numbers in a meaningful way so they can be retrieved later.

Figure 1-1

1. Numbers as Pictures

Memorize in Minutes: The Times Tables uses a picture to represent each number from two to nine. Each picture rhymes with the number it represents and also contains that number. For example, look at the picture that represents the number three. *(Figure 1-1)* Students use a tree to remember the number three. 'Three' rhymes with 'tree.' Notice the picture of the tree also contains the digit three.

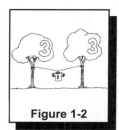

Figure 1-2

The answer to each multiplication fact is another picture based on the combination of the two numbers. Look at the picture used to remember 3 x 3 = 9. *(Figure 1-2)* When a student sees two threes, he or she pictures two trees. Between the two trees, the student visualizes a clothesline. 'Line' rhymes with the answer, 'nine.'

When using the pictures and stories in Memorize in Minutes: The Times Tables, it is as easy for a student to remember 2 x 2 as it is to remember 7 x 8. Each fact is just a different picture.

2. Learning Styles

Every person has an optimum way of learning new information. Memorize in Minutes: The Times Tables presents each multiplication fact using the three basic modalities. Each lesson uses pictures for the visual learner. Stories are used to help the auditory learner. The lesson ends with an activity for the kinesthetic learner who learns by moving, doing, and touching.

3. Multiplication Basics

This book makes it easy for students to remember the multiplication facts, yet it is still extremely important students understand the concept behind the multiplication facts. **Be sure to use the first four lessons with your students.** These lessons are imperative for a complete understanding of multiplication.

Memorize in Minutes: The Times Tables is only a tool in teaching students the multiplication facts. Use your talents as a teacher to make each picture meaningful and the stories interesting.

Why Memorize in Minutes Works

Memorize in Minutes: The Times Tables uses mnemonic devices to help students remember. Mnemonics help transfer information from short term memory to long term memory. To see how this works, let us take a few minutes to understand how the memory process works.

The amount of information the brain can hold is staggering. The average brain contains tens of billions of neurons capable of storing an unbelievable amount of information. Although the brain can hold a tremendous amount of information, it is bombarded by millions of pieces of information every second and is not capable of storing it all.

To keep from being overloaded with information, the brain evaluates, compares, and either stores or ignores each piece of information it receives.

As you are reading this sentence, your brain is collecting a constant stream of information from your senses. Your eyes are seeing the shapes of the letters on the page, comparing these letters and letter combinations with letters and letter combinations stored in memory. As it compares the words with words it has stored, it stores the new information, not as a series of words, but as new pieces of information. Your eyes are also 'seeing' colors and shapes around this book, but your brain is ignoring most of these.

At the same time, your other senses are also collecting information. Your ears are hearing sounds and sending these sounds to the brain. Your brain compares these sounds to bits of information it has stored and chooses to ignore most of them. Yet, if the telephone were to ring, your brain would compare that sound to information it has stored and would probably choose to acknowledge it.

Your nose is collecting information and sending it to the brain also. Again your brain chooses to ignore most of this input. If your nose 'smelled' smoke, your brain would instantly spring into action. The same is true for your sense of touch.

The brain collects information from the senses, compares this information with bits of information stored in the neurons, and then chooses to ignore or store it.

Memory

Memory is nothing more than a record of events picked up by the senses and stored in the brain. These memories are stored for a length of time ranging from just a few seconds to a lifetime. Although there are a number of theories on how the brain actually stores information, many scientists now feel there are three types of memory:
- immediate memory
- short-term memory
- long-term memory

1. Immediate Memory

Immediate memory lasts from just an instant to a few seconds and is also called sensory memory. It is the memory used while the brain is making comparisons and deciding whether to ignore or store the information. It allows us to do continuous activities and make instant comparisons.

2. Short term Memory

A person is able to recall the information stored in short term memory from a few seconds to a few days. The information in short term memory appears to be stored indefinitely. Although stored in the neurons forever, you can only retrieve it for a short time.

Short term memory could be compared to 'finding a needle in a haystack.' Let's say you were sewing while sitting on a haystack. If you were to lay a needle down next to you, you would have a good chance of finding it a minute or two later. But if you left it there for a few hours or a few days, it would be very difficult to find. The information recorded in the neurons in short term memory is the same way. The memory is recorded there, but it is hard to find among the billions of neurons.

Most people have experienced the perils of short term memory while trying to find the television remote control. Where you put the remote is stored in your brain, but the problem lies in recalling that small bit of information.

3. Long-term Memory

Long-term memory is information we can recall for a long time. The difference between long-term memory and short-term memory involves how our brain files the information among the neurons. When our brain just stores the information anywhere among our neurons, it is difficult to retrieve. But when our brain 'links' the information among neurons, the information is much easier to remember.

There appears to be no limit to the amount of information we can store in long term memory or the length of time we can remember it. The key to memory lies in 'linking' new memories to existing memories.

Recall

When memory fails, it is not because we forget. It fails because we didn't put the information into our neurons in a way that is easy to retrieve. It is stored in our brain, we just can't find it.

If we were to put books randomly in a library, it would be very difficult to find any particular book. A library is organized with similar books placed together in an organized manner. This makes finding any specific book easy. The same holds true with your memory. Your mental 'library' must be organized. The better the organization, the easier it will be to recall the information.

There are two different ways to recall information. One is basic recall. In basic recall, the memory just returns. It pops into your head for no apparent reason.

The other type of recall is recognition. Most memory is recognition. In recognition, something triggers the memory. If I were to say 'rabbit,' the word 'rabbit' triggers the part of your brain that stores information about a rabbit. 'Poof,' you recall all types of information about a rabbit. Your brain went to the section of your mental library that contained books on animals, scanned along the books until it found one about rabbits, and slid out the correct book. All this took place almost instantaneously.

Rote Memory

Through the years, most teachers relied on their students' learning of the multiplication facts using rote memory. Rote memory involves repeating each fact over and over again until the student 'remembers' it. What in effect the student is doing is putting the information on many neurons in the brain. The student is putting many needles in the haystack. This is inefficient because the haystack is really large.

Most students eventually learn the multiplication facts, not because they repeat them hundreds of times, but because the brain is finally able to file the similar facts.

Mnemonics

For years, teachers have used mnemonic devices to help students remember. These memory tricks make remembering and make learning fun.

Memorize in Minutes: The Times Tables uses three mnemonic devices to make learning the multiplication facts much easier. It uses **pictures** which rhyme with numbers, **stories** to make the pictures vivid, and **activities** to add kinesthetic qualities.

Teaching Strategies

The techniques presented in Memorize in Minutes: The Times Tables can be presented using one of three techniques, depending on the students with whom you are working and your teaching style and preferences.

1. One Fact a Day

The first technique is to teach Memorize in Minutes: The Times Tables for five to ten minutes a day. Teach one or two new facts each day, and spend plenty of time reviewing the previous multiplication facts. Learning one or two facts a day, coupled with daily review, guarantees all of the students in your class a mastery of the multiplication facts. Although it takes a few months, it is a very effective approach.

2. Attack the Facts

Some teachers like to attack the multiplication facts all at once. In this method, teachers teach five or more multiplication facts each day. If you use this approach, remember to spend ample time reviewing.

3. Supplement

Another approach is to teach most of the multiplication facts the way you have always taught them and use Memorize in Minutes: The Times Tables for only those facts the students are unable to remember. Teachers in the upper grades have used this approach successfully with students who learned many of the facts.

Lasting Memories

For your students to have lasting memories, follow these basic memorizing tips.

1. Pay Attention

Students need to pay attention during lessons. Sometimes, memory is more a problem of *attention* than of *retention*.

2. Use Your Imagination

The more vivid and creative the picture is in the student's mind, the better he or she will remember it. Use your imagination to make the pictures and stories come alive.

3. Use Your Senses

The more senses you can involve, the easier it is for students to recall the memory. Try to make each lesson contain verbal, visual, and kinesthetic qualities.

4. Take it Slowly and Review Often

You are building the foundation for further mathematics. To make this foundation strong, you must **take it slowly and review often**. The more times a student retrieves a memory, the easier it is to retrieve it the next time. This is one area of the curriculum where it does not hurt to over teach the concept. **Remember, slow and steady wins the race.**

5. Have Fun

Memorize in Minutes: The Times Tables can be fun for you and your students. The more fun they have with the pictures, stories, and activities, the easier it will be for them to remember the multiplication facts.

Chapter 2
Detailed Lesson Plans

Materials:
☐ Pre-Test (Page 140)
   Answer Key (Page 154)
☐ Student Record Charts
   (Pages 221 and 222)

Pre-Test

Introduce

Objective:

This test will be used as a benchmark for further progress. The teacher will be able to measure how well each student knows the multiplication facts.

Preparation:

Have students spread their desks apart, or move to where they are not tempted to share answers. Pass out the pre-test. Have students keep the papers face down until you say to begin.

Present

Today you will be taking a test of the basic multiplication facts. Do as many problems as you can. Start with number one and go across the page. Don't worry if you don't know the answer, just go to the next one. Try to do your best. When you are finished, you may correct your answers or sit quietly until the time is up.

Are there any questions? Answer basic questions.

You may begin. Check the time. Students have six minutes to finish the test.

After six minutes . . .

Stop! Collect the papers.

Evaluate

Correct the tests. Use the answer guide on page 154.

It is easy to fill out the *Student Record Charts* located on pages 221 and 222. Make a copy of these pages. Then, put the students names in the vertical column. Next, look at the pre-test. The first 36 facts are all of the multiplication facts except the 0's and 1's. These facts are the multiplication facts taught in this book. A dark line separates the first 36 facts from the rest of the test. There is an order to the first 36 facts. Start with problem 28 (2 x 2), it is the first fact on the *Student Record Chart*. The next fact, 2 x 3, is directly above it. The facts go in sequence up the page. When you reach the top, go one column to the right. The facts continue in sequence down the page to the dark line, then over one column and up the next. This progression continues through the first 36 problems. (The first 36 facts are the only ones you will record on the chart.) Problems 37 through 90 contain the 0's, 1's, and repeats.

As you snake your way through the problems, put a mark in the column of the *Student Record Chart* for each fact that a student misses. Put the mark in the upper left section of the box. The lower right section is for the post-test score. The chart will compare the students' starting score with their final scores.

Pre-Test　　　　　　　　　　　　　　Student Record Chart

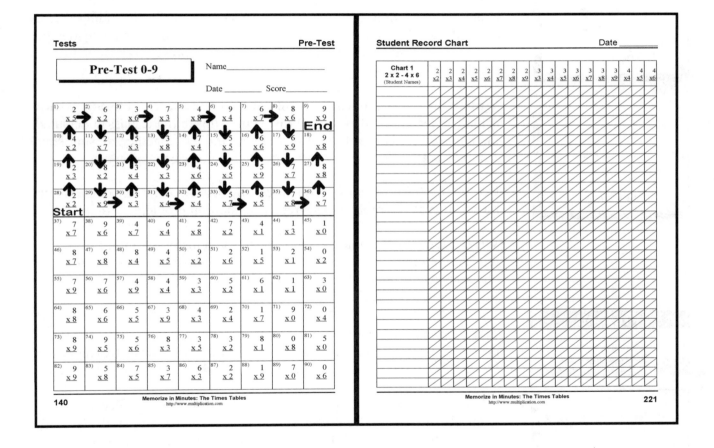

Materials:
- ❑ Small Candy - M &M's or Skittles work well.
- ❑ Student Book (Pages 6 and 7)

Multiplication
Repeated Addition

Introduce:

4
x 3
─────
12

Figure 2-1

Objective:
Students will understand multiplication is a quick form of repeated addition.

Preparation:
Put the multiplication problem 4 x 3 on the board. Lead a general discussion about multiplication. Multiplying numbers is a quick way of adding a series of numbers. The multiplication problem 4 x 3 is actually four added together three times. Use small circles on the board to represent the value of each number. (*Figure 2-1*)

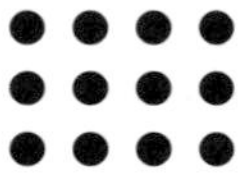

7   7
7   7
x 3   +7
─────   ─────
21   21

Figure 2-2

Write a few more problems on the board and use circles to show what is actually happening. (6 x 2, 5 x 4) Keep doing this until the class understands the concept. It is best to multiply small numbers together. Using small numbers is faster and easier for students to compare the answers.

Next, write the problem 7 x 3 on the board. Instead of making circles on the board, rewrite the problem as a repeated addition problem. (*Figure 2-2*)

Write a few more problems on the board demonstrating multiplication as repeated addition. (8 x 3, 6 x 4) Again, do this until you feel the class understands the concept.

Present:

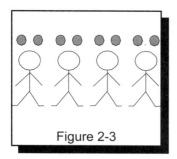

Figure 2-3

Tell the students you are thinking of passing out candy to some students in the class, but you are having a hard time figuring out how many candies are needed. You aren't sure if there will be enough.

If two candies were to be given to four students, how many pieces of candy would be needed? Draw four stick figures representing students on the board. Above each stick figure, draw two circles representing the candy. *(Figure 2-3)* Have the students figure out how many pieces of candy would be needed. Hopefully, they will come up with eight. Reward those who got it right with a piece of candy. *I guarantee the class will be focused on the next multiplication problem!*

Do a few more problems just like the one above. Have the students work the problems out on paper. They should draw stick figures just like you did, with circles representing the pieces of candy.

It is extremely important for students to understand the concept behind multiplication!

When they have grasped the concept, ask them how many candies will be needed to give everybody in the class three pieces of candy. Have them draw a stick figure for each student in the class. Then, they should draw three circles above each student and count the circles. To see if they got the right answer, go around the room giving each student three pieces of candy. Count each as it is given to the student. When the last student is given a third piece of candy, you will have the answer. Ask the students how many had the correct answer on their papers.

Evaluate:

By going through the exercises listed above, the teacher will have a very good idea which students understand the concept. Students do not need to understand multiplication is repeated addition to learn the multiplication facts, yet it is important for a solid math foundation.

Student Book

The multiplication facts are really just a quick way of adding. The multiplication fact 3 x 5 really means 3 + 3 + 3 + 3 + 3.

If you add 3 + 3 + 3 + 3 + 3, your answer is 15. So, the multiplication fact 3 x 5 also equals 15.

Remember: Multiplication is just a quick way of adding.

Page 6

Multiplication
Repeated Addition

$$
\begin{array}{r}
3 \\
3 \\
3 \\
3 \\
+\ 3 \\
\hline
15
\end{array}
$$

• • •
• • •
• • •
• • •
• • •

OR

3 x 5 = 15

Page 7

Materials:
❑ Pair of Dice
❑ Student Book (Pages 8 and 9)

Commutative Property
Of Multiplication

Introduce

Objective:
Students will understand the commutative property of multiplication. When the two numbers being multiplied are reversed, the answer is the same.

Review:
Review the concept discussed in the last lesson, which was multiplication is repeated addition. Demonstrate a few problems on the board.

Present

Write the problem 4 x 3 on the board. Draw three groups of four circles. The answer is twelve. (*Figure 2-4*)

Next, write the problem 3 x 4 on the board. Draw four groups of three circles. The answer is the same twelve. (*Figure 2-5*)

Demonstrate more problems until the students have grasped the concept of the commutative property of multiplication.

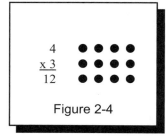

Figure 2-4

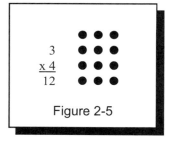

Figure 2-5

Activities:
Dice Count - Roll a pair of dice. Have students stand up in sets that represent each die. If you rolled a 2 and a 4 you would write 2 + 2 + 2 + 2 and 2 x 4 on the board. Then have four groups of two students stand up. Count the students and write the answer on the board next to the problems. Have them sit down. Write 4 + 4 and 4 x 2 on the board. Have two groups of four students stand up. Count the students and write the answers next to the problems on the board. Keep rolling the dice, writing the problem on the board, and having students stand up until they have mastered the concept.

Have the students write down three examples of the commutative property of multiplication.

Student Book

The commutative property simply means it does not matter which number is first when you write the problem. The answer will be the same.

$$3 \times 5 = 15$$
and
$$5 \times 3 = 15$$

In addition, adding 3 five times will give you the same answer as adding 5 three times.

$$3 + 3 + 3 + 3 + 3 = 15$$
and
$$5 + 5 + 5 = 15$$

Page 8

Commutative Property
Of Multiplication

```
  3   ● ● ●
  3   ● ● ●
  3   ● ● ●
  3   ● ● ●
+ 3   ● ● ●
 15
```

is the same as

```
  5   ● ● ● ● ●
  5   ● ● ● ● ●
+ 5   ● ● ● ● ●
 15
```

Page 9

Materials:
❑ Quick Quiz 1 (Page 145)
❑ Small candies
❑ Student Book (Pages 10 and 11)

Multiplication Facts
0's and 1's

Introduce

Objective:
Students will learn the zero and one multiplication facts.

Review:
Review multiplication as repeated addition. (Lesson 2, Pages 16-17) Review the Commutative Property of Multiplication. (Lesson 3, Pages 18-19)

Present

Put the multiplication problem 0 x 3 on the board. Explain to the students 0 x 3 is actually zero added together three times. (*Figure 2-6*)

Lead a discussion with the students about adding zero together. Keep demonstrating problems on the board until the students realize how simple the zero times tables are.

Write 1 x 4 on the board. Ask the students if they can tell how 1 x 4 can be written as an addition problem. They should be able to tell you 1 x 4 is really one added together four times or one four. Write it on the board. *(Figure 2-7)*

Tell the students that multiplying by one is very easy. Any number times one is that number. Also, because of the commutative property of multiplication, one times any number is also that number.

0	0
0	0
x 3	+ 0
0	0
Figure 2-6	

	1
	1
1	1
x 4	+ 1
4	4
Figure 2-7	

Activity:
Candy Count - Write the multiplication fact 0 x 5 on the board. Ask the students to explain what repeated addition problem this stands for. Write the repeated addition fact 0 + 0 + 0 + 0 + 0 on the board. Take out the package of small candy and ask the class if you should give 5 students zero pieces of candy or should you give zero students five pieces of candy. You can work through a few more problems on the board, but it will not take them long to

---

get the picture that any number times zero is nothing.

You can play this same game using the ones multiplication facts. Again, they will gather some valuable insights when five people get one piece of candy, or one person gets five pieces of candy.

Evaluate

Have students sit where they are not tempted to share answers and have them take *Quiz 1* located on page 145. Please refer to page 139, *Taking Quizzes and Tests*, for detailed instructions on correcting, grading, and recording quiz scores.

Student Book

The zeros and ones multiplication facts are very easy.

0's
Any number times zero is always zero. When you think of it as repeated addition, it is just as easy. The multiplication fact 0 x 5 means zero added together five times or $0 + 0 + 0 + 0 + 0$.

1's
Any number multiplied by one is itself. The multiplication fact 6 x 1 means six added one time or six. Or, using the commutative property 6 x 1 is the same as 1 x 6, which means one added together six times or six.

Page 10

Multiplication Facts
0's and 1's

$$
\begin{array}{ccccccc}
6 & 0 & 9 & 0 & 5 & 0 & 7 \\
\times 0 & \times 2 & \times 0 & \times 4 & \times 0 & \times 3 & \times 0 \\
\hline
0 & 0 & 0 & 0 & 0 & 0 & 0
\end{array}
$$
(WOW, the zeros are EASY!)

$$
\begin{array}{ccccccc}
8 & 1 & 1 & 5 & 3 & 4 & 1 \\
\times 1 & \times 2 & \times 9 & \times 1 & \times 1 & \times 1 & \times 6 \\
\hline
8 & 2 & 9 & 5 & 3 & 4 & 6
\end{array}
$$
(The ones are EASY also!)

Page 11

Materials:
❑ Large Flash Cards
❑ Multiplication Fact Charts
   (Page 23)
❑ Student Book (Pages 12 and 13)

Multiplication Facts
Overview

Introduce

Objective:
The students will learn they only need to memorize thirty-six facts out of the one hundred multiplication facts.

Review:
Review *Multiplication as Repeated Addition* (Lesson 2, Pages 16-17), the *Commutative Property of Multiplication* (Lesson 3, Pages 18-19), and the zero and one multiplication facts (Lesson 4, Pages 20-21.)

Present

Make an overhead transparency of *Multiplication Fact Chart 1* located on page 23. Display it on the overhead projector. Explain to the students there are one hundred basic multiplication facts. Take some time to explain that the basic multiplication facts are extremely important.

The multiplication facts are building blocks for mathematics. A student who has not learned the multiplication facts has difficulty succeeding in almost all areas of mathematics. Knowing the multiplication facts is a necessity for much of the math taught above the third grade. The multiplication facts are used in multiplication, division, and fractions.

Show your students that because of the commutative property of multiplication, they do not need to remember all the multiplication facts. Show them forty-five of the multiplication facts are repeats. The repeats are shaded on *Chart 1*.

Put *Chart 2* on the overhead projector. Explain to the students they already know the zero and one multiplication facts. These facts and the repeats are shaded. Out of the one hundred multiplication facts, there are only thirty-six more to learn. Tell them you are going to teach them a fun and easy way to remember those thirty-six multiplication facts.

These charts are also found on pages 12 and 13 of the student book.

Multiplication Fact Chart (With Repeats Shaded)

	0	1	2	3	4	5	6	7	8	9
0	0 x 0	1 x 0	2 x 0	3 x 0	4 x 0	5 x 0	6 x 0	7 x 0	8 x 0	9 x 0
1	0 x 1	1 x 1	2 x 1	3 x 1	4 x 1	5 x 1	6 x 1	7 x 1	8 x 1	9 x 1
2	0 x 2	1 x 2	2 x 2	3 x 2	4 x 2	5 x 2	6 x 2	7 x 2	8 x 2	9 x 2
3	0 x 3	1 x 3	2 x 3	3 x 3	4 x 3	5 x 3	6 x 3	7 x 3	8 x 3	9 x 3
4	0 x 4	1 x 4	2 x 4	3 x 4	4 x 4	5 x 4	6 x 4	7 x 4	8 x 4	9 x 4
5	0 x 5	1 x 5	2 x 5	3 x 5	4 x 5	5 x 5	6 x 5	7 x 5	8 x 5	9 x 5
6	0 x 6	1 x 6	2 x 6	3 x 6	4 x 6	5 x 6	6 x 6	7 x 6	8 x 6	9 x 6
7	0 x 7	1 x 7	2 x 7	3 x 7	4 x 7	5 x 7	6 x 7	7 x 7	8 x 7	9 x 7
8	0 x 8	1 x 8	2 x 8	3 x 8	4 x 8	5 x 8	6 x 8	7 x 8	8 x 8	9 x 8
9	0 x 9	1 x 9	2 x 9	3 x 9	4 x 9	5 x 9	6 x 9	7 x 9	8 x 9	9 x 9

Chart 1

Multiplication Fact Chart (With Repeats, O's and 1's Shaded)

	0	1	2	3	4	5	6	7	8	9
0	0 x 0	1 x 0	2 x 0	3 x 0	4 x 0	5 x 0	6 x 0	7 x 0	8 x 0	9 x 0
1	0 x 1	1 x 1	2 x 1	3 x 1	4 x 1	5 x 1	6 x 1	7 x 1	8 x 1	9 x 1
2	0 x 2	1 x 2	2 x 2	3 x 2	4 x 2	5 x 2	6 x 2	7 x 2	8 x 2	9 x 2
3	0 x 3	1 x 3	2 x 3	3 x 3	4 x 3	5 x 3	6 x 3	7 x 3	8 x 3	9 x 3
4	0 x 4	1 x 4	2 x 4	3 x 4	4 x 4	5 x 4	6 x 4	7 x 4	8 x 4	9 x 4
5	0 x 5	1 x 5	2 x 5	3 x 5	4 x 5	5 x 5	6 x 5	7 x 5	8 x 5	9 x 5
6	0 x 6	1 x 6	2 x 6	3 x 6	4 x 6	5 x 6	6 x 6	7 x 6	8 x 6	9 x 6
7	0 x 7	1 x 7	2 x 7	3 x 7	4 x 7	5 x 7	6 x 7	7 x 7	8 x 7	9 x 7
8	0 x 8	1 x 8	2 x 8	3 x 8	4 x 8	5 x 8	6 x 8	7 x 8	8 x 8	9 x 8
9	0 x 9	1 x 9	2 x 9	3 x 9	4 x 9	5 x 9	6 x 9	7 x 9	8 x 9	9 x 9

Chart 2

Materials:
❑ Student Book (Pages 14 & 15)

Remembering
With Pictures

Introduce

Objective:
Students will understand pictures are easier to remember than numbers.

Review:
Review the material covered in lessons two through four. (Pages 16-23)

Present

Lead a discussion with the students about how the brain remembers information. Be sure to read the *Introduction* on pages 7-12.

Close your eyes. How many of you can see a tree? Ask for a show of hands. **Your brain can see pictures easily. With your eyes closed can you see: a horse, a piano, a giraffe, a hamburger, etc? Isn't it neat how these pictures just pop into your head? Your brain is able to see and remember all kinds of pictures.** Go through as many examples as needed for the students to realize how easy it is to see pictures in their heads.

Although you are not looking at real pictures of the animals or objects, you can easily see the pictures in your head. You can see the pictures mentally. It is as if your brain is connected to a television set you can watch in your head.

Not only do you have a built-in television, but you also have a built-in video cassette recorder (VCR). You can play back the pictures any time you want. Once you see a picture, your brain stores it away, and can retrieve it anytime you wish.

Close your eyes again and picture a cat. What color is the cat you picture? Does it have long hair or short hair? Have a general discussion. **How many of you can close your eyes and see a green cat? How about a purple cat? Can you see a cat that is as big as a tree?** Have discussion about all the funny ways you can see a cat in your mind.

Your brain can take pictures and see them in all types of funny ways. Your brain remembers funny pictures easier than it remembers pictures that are not funny.

As a review of today's discussion, read pages 14 and 15 with your students.

Evaluate

As you discuss with your students, you should have a good idea of how well your students have grasped the concept of seeing pictures.

Student Book

Your brain operates like a television set and you can see pictures anytime you want. It even operates when you are asleep, showing you dreams. Pictures are easy for your brain to remember and numbers are more difficult to remember. In this book you will learn the multiplication facts using pictures instead of numbers.

Besides having a built-in television, you also have a built-in VCR that can play back pictures any time you want. Once you see a picture, your brain stores it away and can play it back later.

Your brain remembers funny pictures better than it remembers regular pictures. In this book, you will be using funny stories to remember the multiplication facts.

Remembering
With Pictures

Page 14

Page 15

Materials:
❑ Large Flash Cards 2 - 6
❑ Student Book (Pages 16 & 17)

Numbers 2 - 6
Mental Pictures

Introduce

Objective:
Students will develop mental pictures for the numbers 2 - 6.

Review:
Review how to remember with funny pictures.

Present

Using a picture of each number, have students develop mental pictures of each. Remember, for students to succeed in remembering the multiplication facts they need to memorize each of the pictures two through nine.

Shoe

2 = Shoe
Show the students the picture of the shoe. *(Large Flash Card 2, page 169)* Shoe rhymes with two. Explain to them every time they see the number two, you want them to think shoe. Point out the two in the picture of the shoe. Have them close their eyes and see if they can see a shoe.

Tree

3 = Tree
Tree rhymes with three. Show students the picture of the tree. *(Large Flash Card 3, page 169)* Show the students the tree actually has a three in it. Have them close their eyes and see the tree with a three in it.

Quiz students on three and two using the Large Flash Cards.

Door

4 = Door
Hold up the picture of the door. *(Large Flash Card 4, page 171)* Show them that the door has a four in it. Have them close their eyes and see the door. To help build a good mental picture, some teachers use construction paper to put a big four on their classroom door.

*Use the Large Flash Cards to quiz students on two, three, and four. When you hold up the four, they should say 'door.' Do this for each number. **Resist the temptation to teach too much, too fast. You want 100% of the students to learn 100% of the multiplication facts. IT TAKES TIME!***

Hive

5 = Hive
Show the students the picture of the hive. *(Large Flash Card 5, page 171)* Have them close their eyes and see a bee hive. Tell them how the hive will remind them of five. They rhyme. Some students will not know what a bee

---

Chick

hive is. Take some time to discuss with them what a bee hive is and what it is used for.

Quiz students on two, three, four, and five using the Large Flash Cards.

6 = Chick
Show the students the picture of the chick that represents the number six. *(Large Flash Card 6, page 173)* Discuss with them that every time they hear or see six, they should think of a chick. Have them close their eyes and see a chick.

Evaluate

Buzz: The game Buzz uses a different motion for each number. When you say each number the students will respond with the appropriate motion.

Two   - students point at their shoes.
Three - students pretend to be a pine tree. Both arms straight, pointing downward, hands away from their bodies.
Four   - students pretend to knock on a door.
Five   - students buzz.
Six   - students pretend they are chicks and flap their wings.

Have the students close their eyes. Say the number 4. Students should pretend to knock. Continue to go through the numbers in random order.

Around the World *[Instructions on page 167]*: Play Around the World using the large flash cards. Have the student say the picture he or she remembers.

Student Book

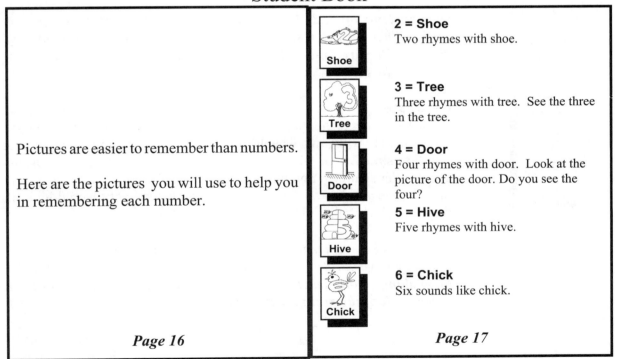

Pictures are easier to remember than numbers.

Here are the pictures you will use to help you in remembering each number.

2 = Shoe
Two rhymes with shoe.

Shoe

3 = Tree
Three rhymes with tree. See the three in the tree.

Tree

4 = Door
Four rhymes with door. Look at the picture of the door. Do you see the four?

Door

5 = Hive
Five rhymes with hive.

Hive

6 = Chick
Six sounds like chick.

Chick

Page 16   *Page 17*

Materials:
❑ Large Flash Cards 2 - 9
❑ Student Book (Pages 18 & 19)

Numbers 7 - 9
Mental Pictures

Introduce

Objective:
Students will develop mental pictures for the numbers 7 - 9.

Review:
Review the mental pictures the students developed for the numbers 2 - 6.

Present

Use pictures to help students develop mental pictures for the numbers 7, 8, and 9.

Surfin'

7 = Surfin'

Show students the surfin' picture. *(Large Flash Card 7, page 173)* Show them the surfboard on top of the wave. Describe surfing to your students. Explain that surfing will remind them of the number seven. Point out how the wave looks like a number seven. Instead of surfing, have them remember the slang word surfin'. Depending on the experiences of your students and your geographic location, you may need to spend more time helping them develop a good mental picture of surfing.

Quiz students on 2, 3, 4, 5, 6, and 7. Use the back of the large number cards. When a student sees a number, you want him or her to think of the picture. Be sure to hold up the number and have the student say the name of the picture he or she sees.

Skate

8 = Skate

Show the students the picture of the skate. *(Large Flash Card 8, page 175)* Show them how the two wheels of the skate form an eight when the skate is standing straight up. Help paint a visual picture by leading a discussion about roller skating. You might want to describe your experiences or those of someone you know. Have them draw what an eight would look like if they thought of roller blades rather than skates.

*Use the back of the large flash cards to quiz students on two through eight. Remember, when you hold up the eight, they should say "skate." **Don't rush them along. Don't teach too much, too fast. You want all of the students to learn all of the multiplication facts.***

9 = Sign

Hold up the picture of the sign. *(Large Flash Card 9, page 175)* Show them on the picture how the sign contains the number nine. Have them close their eyes and see a sign. Sign rhymes with nine. From now on, every time your students see nine, they should think sign.

Duplicate the picture side of the *Large Flash Cards 2 - 9 located on pages 169-175.* Have students color each card. *[Activity 17, Page 134]* These, along with the multiplication facts that follow, can be compiled into a coloring book.

Evaluate

Even though all the students have mastered the pictures for the numbers, still take a few minutes each day to reinforce the pictures by quizzing them with one of the games. (You may also use the games when you have a few spare minutes during the day.)

Quiz the students over the numbers 2 through 9. For <u>Memorize in Minutes: The Times Tables</u> to work to its potential, students need to 'see' the picture for each number.

Play the games described in Lesson 7 on page 27 until **all** students have mastered the mental pictures. When playing **Buzz**, the actions are as follows:

Seven - Students pretend to surf. They act like they are balancing on a surf board.

Eight - Students put both hands behind their back and pretend to skate. (Sliding feet in a skating motion.)

Nine - Students put both arms above their head, elbow out, pretending they are a sign.

Student Book

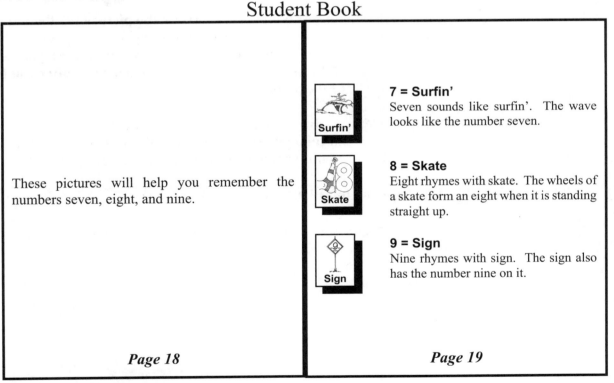

These pictures will help you remember the numbers seven, eight, and nine.

7 = Surfin'
Seven sounds like surfin'. The wave looks like the number seven.

8 = Skate
Eight rhymes with skate. The wheels of a skate form an eight when it is standing straight up.

9 = Sign
Nine rhymes with sign. The sign also has the number nine on it.

Page 18   *Page 19*

Materials:
❑ Picture Quiz 1 (Page 141)
❑ Crayons (Optional)

Review 1
Quiz on pictures 2 through 9

Introduce

Objective:
Check student recall of the picture for each number 2 through 9.

Preparation:
Have the students spread their desks apart or move to where they are not tempted to share answers. Pass out a copy of *Picture Quiz 1* (Page 141) to each student.

Introduction:
Today you will be taking a quiz over the pictures you have learned for each of the numbers two through nine. This quiz is a picture quiz. You are to draw the picture you see in your head that goes with each number.

Present

At the top of the page, please write your name and the date.

Look at the upper left box. It says, "Draw the picture for the number two." When I say, "Begin," draw the picture you see in your mind for number two. Draw a picture in each of the boxes. If you don't remember one of the pictures, skip it and come back to it after you have drawn the rest of the pictures.

Take your time to draw each picture with detail. If you finish before I say stop, you can take out your color crayons and color the pictures. You will have ten minutes to complete the drawings.

Are there any questions? Answer basic questions.

You may begin. Check the time. Students have ten minutes to complete the quiz.

After ten minutes . . .

Stop. Collect and score the papers.

Tests   **Picture Quiz 1**

Picture Quiz 1

Name_____

Date _____   Score_____

Draw the picture for the number **2**.	Draw the picture for the number **3**.	Draw the picture for the number **4**.
Draw the picture for the number **5**.	Draw the picture for the number **6**.	Draw the picture for the number **7**.
Draw the picture for the number **8**.	Draw the picture for the number **9**.	

Memorize in Minutes: The Times Tables
http://www.multiplication.com
141

Materials:
❑ Large Flash Cards
❑ Coloring Page 2 x 2 (Page 177)
❑ Student Book (Pages 20 & 21)

FACT 2 x 2 = 4
Shoe x Shoe = Floor

Introduce

Objective:
Students will learn the multiplication fact 2 x 2 = 4.

Review:
Review the pictures for each number two through nine. Use the large flash cards for 2 through 9 or play the "Buzz Game," directions on page 27.

Preparation:
Write the multiplication fact 2 x 2 on the board and the repeated addition fact 2 + 2 on the board. This is the only multiplication fact that has the same answer as the addition fact.

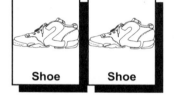

2	2
x 2	+ 2
4	4
Multiplication Fact	**Repeated Addition**

Introduction:
The first multiplication fact you will be learning is 2 x 2 = 4. Two times two is equal to four. Remember that 2 x 2 is actually two added twice, or two groups of two.

When you learn the multiplication facts using pictures, it is important to 'see' the picture in your head. When you look at 2 x 2, you should 'see' shoe x shoe or two shoes.

Shoe   Shoe

Present

Story:
A young boy received a new pair of shoes for his birthday. They were just the kind of shoes he had always wanted. When he put them on, he found they were too big.

Even though they did not fit, he decided to wear them to school the next day. Sometimes, as he would walk along, he would step right out of them. He would look down at his feet and be in his socks. The shoes would be sitting on the floor. As you can imagine, this was very embarrassing for the boy.

Shoe x Shoe = Floor

Picture:
Stand up. Look down at your two shoes. Can you imagine what it would be like to have shoes that were too big? Close your eyes and 'see' your two shoes on the floor. This is the picture you will remember to learn the first multiplication fact.

Floor rhymes with four. Seeing two shoes on the floor helps you

remember 2 x 2 = 4 or shoe x shoe = floor. Every time you see 2 x 2, you will 'see' shoe x shoe or two shoes. When you see the two shoes in your mind, you will remember two shoes are on the floor. Floor reminds you of the answer four.

Hold up the picture side of *Large Flash Card 2 x 2.* **This picture may not be as good as the mental picture you saw, but we will use it to help us remember the picture. See the two shoes which are on the floor.**

Activities:
❑ Have the students color the 2 x 2 picture on *Coloring Page 5* located on page 177. *[Activity 17, Page 134]*
❑ Have the students act out the story of the boy walking out of his shoes. *[Activity 1, Page 133]*

Evaluate

Quiz the students over the multiplication fact 2 x 2 and the pictures for the numbers 2 through 9.

Student Book

A young boy received a new pair of shoes for his birthday. They were just the kind of shoes he had always wanted. When he put them on, he found they were too big. Even though they did not fit, he decided to wear them to school the next day. Sometimes, as he would walk along, he would step right out of them. He would look down at his feet and be in his socks. The shoes would be sitting on the floor. As you can imagine, this was very embarrassing for the boy.

Page 20

2 x 2 = 4

Shoe x Shoe = Floor

Page 21

Materials:
- ❑ Large Flash Cards
- ❑ Coloring Page 2 x 3 (Page 177
- ❑ Student Book (Pages 22 & 23)

FACT 2 x 3 = 6
Shoe x Tree = Sticks

Introduce

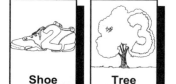

		2	
2	3	2	3
x 3	x 2	+ 2	+ 3
6	6	6	6
Multiplication Fact		Repeated Addition	

Shoe   Tree

Objective:
Students will learn the multiplication facts 2 x 3 = 6 and 3 x 2 = 6.

Review:
Review the pictures two through nine and the multiplication fact 2 x 2.

Preparation:
Write the multiplication facts 2 x 3, 3 x 2, and the repeated addition facts on the board. Discuss with the students that 2 x 3 is a shorthand way of writing 3 + 3, and 3 x 2 is a shorthand way of writing 2 + 2 + 2.

Introduction:
Today we are going to learn the multiplication fact 2 x 3. When you look at the number two, what picture do you 'see?' Shoe. What picture do you 'see' when you think of the number three? Tree. The story I am going to tell you is about a shoe in a tree.

Present

Shoe x Tree = Sticks

Story:
There once were two young birds. They started building a nest because they were going to have their first babies. Building a nest turned out to be hard work. It takes many little sticks to build a nest and it seemed as if the nest would never get finished.

The birds were flying around looking for sticks when the mother bird saw an old shoe lying on the ground. The bird had a great idea. She picked up stick after stick and put them into the shoe. When the shoe was full, the two birds grabbed onto the shoe laces and flew back to the tree, carrying the shoe. When they got to the tree, they tied the shoe to a limb. By moving some of the sticks in the shoe, they quickly had a nest.

Picture:
**Close your eyes and 'see' a tree. Now picture a shoe filled with sticks tied to one of the limbs of the tree. This is the picture that will help you remember that 3 x 2 = 6 and 2 x 3 = 6. Whenever you see 2 x 3, you will remember the picture of a shoe in a tree filled with sticks.
Tree x shoe = sticks or 3 x 2 = 6.**

Show the students the picture of the shoe in the tree filled with sticks. (*Large Flash Card 2 x 3*)

Activities:

❏ Have the students color the 2 x 3 picture on *Coloring Page 5* located on page 177. *[Activity 17, Page 134]*

❏ Have students sculpt the shoe filled with sticks and the tree out of clay. *[Activity 15, Page 134]*

Evaluate

Evaluate how well the class is remembering the facts. Hold-up each fact chart to quiz students on the numbers 2 through 9 and the multiplication facts 2 x 2, 2 x 3, and 3 x 2.

Student Book

There once were two young birds. They started building a nest because they were going to have their first babies. Building a nest turned out to be hard work. It takes many little sticks to build a nest, and it seemed as if the nest would never get finished.

The birds were flying around looking for sticks when the mother bird saw an old shoe lying on the ground. The bird had a great idea. She picked up stick after stick and put them into the shoe. When the shoe was full, the two birds grabbed onto the shoe laces and flew back to the tree, carrying the shoe. When they got to the tree, they tied the shoe to one of its limbs. By moving some of the sticks in the shoe, they quickly had a nest.

Page 22

2 x 3 = 6

Shoe x Tree = Sticks

Page 23

Materials:
❑ Large Flash Cards
❑ Coloring Page 2 x 4 (Page 179)
❑ Student Book (Pages 24 and 25)

FACT 2 x 4 = 8
Shoe x Door = Plate

Introduce

	2		
	2		
2	4	2	4
x 4	x 2	+ 2	+ 4
8	8	8	8
Multiplication Fact		Repeated Addition	

Shoe · Door

Objective:
Students will learn the multiplication facts 2 x 4 = 8 and 4 x 2 =8.

Review:
Review the pictures two through nine and the multiplication facts 2 x 2 and 2 x 3.

Preparation:
Write the multiplication facts 2 x 4, 4 x 2, and the repeated addition facts on the board. Discuss with the students that 2 x 4 is a shorthand way of writing 4 + 4, and 4 x 2 is a shorthand way of writing 2 + 2 + 2 + 2.

Introduction:
Some pictures you will see in your head will be funny. To help us remember 2 x 4, we use a funny picture. Close your eyes. I want you to see a giant shoe, a shoe as big as this room. Do any of you know the story of 'The Old Lady Who Lived in a Shoe?' The story is about an old lady who used a large shoe as her house. She had so many children she didn't know what to do. Discuss the story, 'The Old Lady Who Lived in the Shoe,' with the students.

Present

Shoe x Door = Plate

Story:
There was an old lady who lived in a shoe. She had so many children she didn't know what to do. This lady loved pretty plates. Her children knew she liked pretty plates, so they would each buy her a plate for her birthday and many other holidays. After a while, she had so many plates they did not fit in her cupboards. She had to start stacking them everywhere around her house.

After many years, there were so many plates, when the front door was opened, out would roll plates.

Picture:
Close your eyes and picture the giant shoe again. Picture the old lady stacking plates everywhere. There are plates in the hallway, on the counters, and filling the cupboards. Picture yourself walking up to the front door of the giant shoe. You knock on the door and the lady comes

to the door. As she opens the door, out roll dozens of plates.

This is the picture you want to remember. Whenever you see 2 x 4, you will see a shoe with a door. When you think of a shoe with a door, you will remember the old lady in the shoe and her plates coming out the door. Remember, 2 x 4 = 8 or shoe x door = plate. Show the students the picture of the plates rolling out of the door in the shoe. (*Large Flash Card 2 x 4*)

Activities:
❏ Have the students color the 2 x 4 picture on *Coloring Page 6* located on page 179. *[Activity 17, Page 134]*
❏ Choose an activity which best suits your class from the "Teaching Activities" section (Pages 133-138)

Evaluate

Evaluate as a class. Hold-up each fact chart to quiz students on the numbers 2 through 9 and the multiplication facts 2 x 2, 2 x 3 and 3 x 2.

Student Book

There was an old lady who lived in a shoe. She had so many children she didn't know what to do. This lady loved pretty plates. Her children knew she liked pretty plates, so they would each buy her a plate for her birthday and many other holidays. After a while, she had so many plates they did not fit in her cupboards. She had to start stacking them everywhere around her house. After many years, there were so many plates, when the front door was opened, out would roll plates.	**2 x 4 = 8** **Shoe x Door = Plate**
Page 24	*Page 25*

Materials:
❑ Large Flash Cards
❑ Coloring Page 2 x 5 (Page 179)
❑ Student Book (Pages 26 & 27)

FACT 2 x 5 = 10
Shoe x Hive = Pen

Introduce

2		2	
		2	
		2	
2	5	2	5
x 5	x 2	+ 2	+ 5
10	10	10	10
Multiplication Fact		**Repeated Addition**	

Shoe   Hive

Objective:
Students will learn the multiplication facts 2 x 5 = 10 and 5 x 2 = 10.

Review:
Review the pictures two through nine and the multiplication facts 2 x 2, 2 x 3, and 2 x 4.

Preparation:
Write the multiplication facts 2 x 5 and 5 x 2 and the repeated addition facts on the board. Discuss with the students that 2 x 5 is a shorthand way of writing 5 + 5 and 5 x 2 is a shorthand way of writing 2 + 2 + 2 + 2 + 2.

Introduction:
The next multiplication fact we will be learning is 2 x 5. Two times five is equal to ten. To remember 2 x 5, we will use another silly story.

Present

Shoe x Hive = Pen

Story:
Once upon a time there was a young bee hive who was very forgetful. His friends and parents would tell him things, but he would never remember them. To help him remember, he started to write himself notes, but he could never remember where he had put the notes.

Although he was forgetful, this hive was very clever. The hive bought a special pen that could be erased easily, and he started writing his notes on his shoes. Using his shoes and his special pen, the hive solved his problem.

Picture:
Close your eyes. I want you to see a hive writing on his shoe with his special pen. When you see 5 x 2, you will think a hive and a shoe. When you see 2 x 5, you will also think of a shoe and a hive. When you think of a shoe and a hive, you will remember the story of the hive writing notes on his shoes with the pen. Hive x shoe = pen.

Activities:
❑ Have the students color the 2 x 5 picture on *Coloring Page 6* located on page 179. *[Activity 17, Page 134]*
❑ Choose an activity which best suits your class from the "Teaching Activities" section. (Pages 133-138)

Evaluate

Again quiz your students over the multiplication facts they have learned. Don't be afraid of reviewing too much. You WANT the students to over learn the material. ***Remember, the goal is for ALL of your STUDENTS to know ALL of the multiplication facts.***

Student Book

Once upon a time there was a young bee hive who was very forgetful. His friends and parents would tell him things, but he would never remember them. To help him remember, he started to write himself notes, but he could never remember where he had put the notes. Although he was forgetful, this hive was very clever. The hive bought a special pen that could be erased easily, and he started writing his notes on his shoes. Using his shoes and his special pen, the hive solved his problem.	**2 x 5 = 10**  **Shoe x Hive = Pen**
Page 26	*Page 27*

Materials:
- ❑ Large Flash Cards
- ❑ Coloring Page 2 x 6 (Page 181)
- ❑ Student Book (Pages 28 & 29)

FACT 2 x 6 = 12
Shoe x Chicks = Elf

Introduce

```
        2
        2
        2
        2
  2   6   2   6
 x6  x2  +2  +6
 12  12  12  12
Multiplication  Repeated
    Fact        Addition
```

Shoe   Chick

Objective:
Students will learn the multiplication facts 2 x 6 = 12 and 6 x 2 = 12.

Review:
Review the pictures two through nine and the multiplication facts 2 x 2, 2 x 3, 2 x 4, and 2 x 5.

Preparation:
Write the multiplication facts 2 x 6 and 6 x 2 and the repeated addition fact for each on the board. Discuss with the students that 2 x 6 is a shorthand way of writing 6 + 6 and 6 x 2 is a shorthand way of writing 2 + 2 + 2 + 2 + 2 + 2.

Introduction:
When I say the number two, what picture do you think of? Shoe. **What do you 'see' when you hear the number six?** Chicks.

Do any of you know who Santa's special helpers are? Elves. **What does an elf look like?** A funny hat, pointed ears, funny shoes, etc.

Present

Shoe x Chick = Elf

Story:
A teacher decided to put on a winter play. A chick was chosen to be an elf, one of Santa's special helpers. He was so excited. When he went home that night, his mother made him an elf costume. She made little elf shoes and a little elf hat. He put them on and was very proud.

During the play, the chick helped Santa deliver presents to good boys and girls. The chick had fun pretending he was an elf.

Picture:
Whenever you see 2 x 6, you will remember a shoe and a chick. I want you to close your eyes and see a chick dressed like an elf. He has elf shoes on. When you think of a chick with shoes, you will remember an elf, which will remind you of the answer, 12.

Show the students the chick dressed like an elf. *(Large Flash Card 2 x 6)* **This is the picture you will use to help remember 2 x 6 = 12.**

Activity:
❑ Have the students color the 2 x 6 picture on *Coloring Page 7* located on page 181. *[Activity 17, Page 134]*
❑ This is a great story to act out. *[Activity 1, Page 133]*
❑ Choose an activity which best suits your class from the "Teaching Activities" section. (Pages 133-138)

Evaluate

Again quiz your students over the multiplication facts they have learned.

Student Book

A teacher decided to put on a winter play. A chick was chosen to be an elf, one of Santa's special helpers. He was so excited. When he went home that night, his mother made him an elf costume. She made little elf shoes and a little elf hat. He put them on and was very proud.

During the play, the chick helped Santa deliver presents to good boys and girls. The chick had fun pretending he was an elf.

Page 28

2 x 6 = 12

Shoe x Chick = Elf

Page 29

Materials:
- ❑ Large Flash Cards
- ❑ Coloring Page 2 x 7 (Page 181)
- ❑ Student Book (Pages 30 & 31)

FACT 2 x 7 = 14
Shoe x Surfin' = Four Kings

Introduce

Multiplication Fact	Repeated Addition

Objective:
Students will learn the multiplication facts 2 x 7 = 14 and 7 x 2 = 14.

Review:
Review the pictures two through nine and the multiplication facts 2 x 2, 2 x 3, 2 x 4, 2 x 5, and 2 x 6.

Preparation:
Write the multiplication facts 2 x 7 and 7 x 2 and the repeated addition fact for each on the board. Discuss with the students that 2 x 7 is a shorthand way of writing 7 + 7 and 7 x 2 is another way of writing 2 + 2 + 2 + 2 + 2 + 2 + 2.

Introduction:
Today you are going to learn a funny picture for remembering another multiplication fact. You will learn the multiplication fact 2 x 7 = 14. When you say seven, what picture pops into your head? Surfin'. **What about the number two?** Shoe.

Here is a funny story about four kings.

Present

Shoe x Surfin' = Four Kings

Story:
Four kings had been friends since they were children. If you looked at three of the kings, you would not see anything unusual about them, except they always wore their crowns. If you saw the fourth king, you would notice something strange. He had giant feet. His feet were so big he needed special shoes. The shoes had to be made just for him.

Each year, the kings went on a vacation together. One year, they went to the beach. They watched the people surfing. It looked like fun, but they did not have surfboards.

The king with the big feet had a funny idea. He thought they could all surf on his enormous shoes. So the four kings swam out into the water and three of the kings got on the shoulders of the king with the enormous shoes. When a wave came, the kings surfed to the beach on the enormous shoes. They had great fun surfing.

Picture:
Whenever you see 2 x 7, you will remember shoe and surfin'. The picture of the four kings will instantly come into your mind. I want you to close your eyes to see four kings surfing. They are surfing on the shoes of the king with giant feet. The two reminds you of shoe. Seven reminds you of surfin.' When you 'see' these in your mind, you will remember the four kings (14).

Show the students the picture of the four surfing kings. *(Large Flash Card 2 x 7)*

Activity:
❏ Have the students color the 2 x 7 picture on *Coloring Page 7* located on page 181. *[Activity 17, Page 134]*
❏ Choose an activity which best suits your class from the "Teaching Activities" section. (Pages 133-138)

Evaluate

Again quiz your students over the multiplication facts they have learned.

Student Book

Four kings had been friends since they were children. If you looked at three of the kings, you would not see anything unusual about them, except they always wore their crowns. If you saw the fourth king, you would notice something strange. He had giant feet. His feet were so big he needed special shoes. The shoes had to be made just for him.

Each year, the kings went on a vacation together. One year, they went to the beach. They watched the people surfing. It looked like fun, but they did not have surfboards.

The king with the big feet had a funny idea. He thought they could all surf on his enormous shoes. So the four kings swam out into the water and three of the kings got on the shoulders of the king with the enormous shoes. When a wave came, the kings surfed to the beach on the enormous shoes. They had great fun surfing.

Page 30

2 x 7 = 14

Shoe x Surfin' = Four Kings

Page 31

Materials:
❏ Large Flash Cards
❏ Coloring Page 2 x 8 (Page 183)
❏ Paper Crown
❏ Student Book (Pages 32 & 33)

FACT 2 x 8 = 16
Shoe x Skate = Sick Queen

Introduce

```
          2
          2
          2
          2
          2
          2
  2   8   2    8
 x 8  x 2 +2   +8
 16   16  16   16
Multiplication  Repeated
    Fact        Addition
```

Shoe   Skate

Objective:
Students will learn the multiplication facts 2 x 8 = 16 and 8 x 2 = 16.

Review:
Review the pictures two through nine and the multiplication facts 2 x 2, 2 x 3, 2 x 4, 2 x 5, 2 x 6, and 2 x 7.

Preparation:
Write the multiplication facts 2 x 8, 8 x 2, and the repeated addition facts on the board, discussing each.

Introduction:
When I say two, what do you see in your mind? A shoe. **When I say eight, what do you see?** A skate. Show students the flash cards to refresh their memories.

Today, I am going to tell you a story about a queen. This queen had always wanted to learn how to roller skate.

Present

Shoe x Skate =
Sick Queen

Story:
Once there was a silly queen. She loved to do things other queens would never think of doing. She wanted to learn how to roller skate. The queen went to a roller skating rink, rented roller skates, and sat down on a bench to take off her shoes. She put a skate on one foot and decided to stand up to see what it felt like to be on a skate. She lost her balance and before she knew what was happening, she started rolling. She rolled out onto the skating rink floor. She tried to stop, but started twirling and twirling and twirling. This made her feel sick. She was a sick queen.

Picture:

Close your eyes. Can you 'see' a queen wearing one shoe and one skate, spinning around so many times she gets sick? This picture will remind you of sixteen. Sick queen sounds like sixteen.

This funny picture will help you remember 2 x 8 = 16. Every time you see a two and an eight, you will remember the shoe and the skate on the sick queen. Remember, 2 x 8 = 16 or shoe times skate equals sick queen.

Show the students the picture of the queen with a shoe on one foot and a skate on the other. *(Large Flash Card 2 x 8)*

Activities:
❑ Have the students color the 2 x 8 picture on *Coloring Page 8* located on page 183. *[Activity 17, Page 134]*
❑ Students act out the story wearing a paper crown.*[Activity 1, Page 133]*
❑ Choose an activity which best suits your class from the "Teaching Activities" section. (Pages 133-138)

Evaluate

Quiz your students over the multiplication facts they have learned.

Student Book

Once there was a silly queen. She loved to do things other queens would never think of doing. She wanted to learn how to roller skate. The queen went to a roller skating rink, rented roller skates, and sat down on a bench to take off her shoes. She put a skate on one foot and decided to stand up to see what it felt like to be on a skate. She lost her balance and before she knew what was happening, she started rolling. She rolled out onto the skating rink floor. She tried to stop, but started twirling and twirling and twirling. This made her feel sick. She was a sick queen.

Page 32

2 x 8 = 16

Shoe x Skate = Sick Queen

Page 33

Materials:
- ❏ Large Flash Cards
- ❏ Coloring Page 2 x 9 (Page 183)
- ❏ Yardstick
- ❏ Student Book (Pages 34 & 35)

FACT 2 x 9 = 18
Shoe x Sign = Aching

Introduce

```
              2
              2
              2
              2
              2
              2
              2
   2      9      2      9
  x 9    x 2    + 2    + 9
  ---    ---    ---    ---
   18    18     18     18
Multiplication   Repeated
    Fact         Addition
```

Shoe   Sign

Objective:
Students will learn the multiplication facts 2 x 9 = 18 and 9 x 2 = 18.

Review:
Review the pictures two through nine and the multiplication facts 2 x 2, 2 x 3, 2 x 4, 2 x 5, 2 x 6, 2 x 7, and 2 x 8.

Preparation:
Write the multiplication facts 2 x 9 and 9 x 2 and the repeated addition facts on the board. Discuss each.

Introduction:
Have you ever had a toothache or a headache? How does it feel when something starts aching? Discuss the word aching. Students need to understand what the term aching means.

We are going to talk about giants today. Imagine if you were a giant. Close your eyes and imagine yourself as a giant. Everyone stand up. OUCH! Your head hit the ceiling. Look down at your shoes. How big would your shoes be if you were a giant? Huge.

This is a story about a giant who had enormous shoes!

Present

Shoe x Sign = Aching

Story:
Once there was a giant. He was really big. He was so big he couldn't go into buildings. It was lonely being a giant. Most people were afraid of him even though he was friendly.

One day he was so lonely he decided to go into the city. Most of the people ran away when they saw him. As he got near the center of town, he noticed some men with yellow hats working. The men did not see him. As he got closer, he could tell they were putting in a new sign. He walked up to the man holding onto the sign, tapped him on the shoulder, and said, "Hello." When the man saw the giant, he was so scared he dropped the sign and ran. The sign landed on the giant's shoe. OUCH! The giant's toe started aching!

Picture:
Show the students the picture of the sign landing on the giants shoe. *(Large Flash Card 2 x 9)*

These are the story and the picture you will use to remember 2 x 9 = 18. A sign falls on your shoe and your toe starts aching. Close your eyes to see the sign falling on your shoe. Two makes you think of a shoe and nine makes you think of a stop sign. When you think of a sign and a shoe, you will remember your toe aching. Aching sounds like 18, and 2 x 9 = 18.

Activities:

❑ Have the students color the 2 x 9 picture on *Coloring Page 8* located on page 183. *[Activity 17, Page 134]*

❑ Students act out the story. You may use a yardstick for the sign. *[Activity 1, Page 133]*

❑ Choose an activity which best suits your class from the "Teaching Activities" section. (Pages 133-138)

Evaluate

Quiz the students over the multiplication facts learned so far. Use *Quick Quiz 2*. (Page 145)

Student Book

Once there was a giant. He was really big. He was so big he couldn't go into buildings. It was lonely being a giant. Most people were afraid of him even though he was friendly.

One day he was so lonely he decided to go into the city. Most of the people ran away when they saw him. As he got near the center of town, he noticed some men with yellow hats working. The men did not see him. As he got closer, he could tell they were putting in a new sign. He walked up to the man holding onto the sign, tapped him on the shoulder, and said, "Hello." When the man saw the giant, he was so scared he dropped the sign and ran. The sign landed on the giant's shoe. OUCH! The giant's toe started aching!

Page 34

2 x 9 = 18

Shoe x Sign = Aching

Page 35

Materials:
❑ Large Flash Cards
❑ Coloring Page 3 x 3 (Page 185)
❑ T-shirt with 9 taped to it or
   Paper cut-out of a shirt
❑ Student Book (Pages 36 & 37)

FACT 3 x 3 = 9
Tree x Tree = Line

Introduce

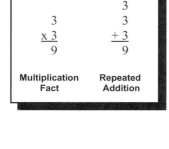

```
        3
  3     3
 x 3   + 3
 ___   ___
  9     9

Multiplication   Repeated
    Fact         Addition
```

Tree   Tree

Objective:
Students will learn the multiplication fact 3 x 3 = 9.

Review:
Reviewing is the key to students remembering the multiplication facts. As you review the twos, have the students draw the pictures they see for each multiplication fact. They should be able to draw a picture for each number and each multiplication fact they have learned.

Preparation:
Write 3 x 3 = 9 on the board. Write the repeated addition problem on the board. Discuss with the students that 3 x 3 is actually a shorthand way of writing three threes or 3 + 3 + 3.

Introduction:
Today we are going to move on to the threes. Show the flash card for the three. **For the next few days you will be remembering pictures that involve trees. How many of you remember a picture we have already learned that has a tree in it?** 2 x 3 = 6

Today you are going to learn a picture that will help you remember 3 x 3 = 9. Draw a large tree on the board. Draw another large tree on the board about 4 feet to the side.

Present

Tree x Tree = Line

Story:
There was a boy who loved to play football with his friends. His parents knew how much he loved football, so they gave him a football jersey to wear. The number on the back was of his favorite professional football player. It was the number nine. *Hold up the T-shirt you brought in with a paper nine taped on it or a shirt cut out of paper with the number nine written on it.*

One day he was playing football with his friends. He was trying to catch a pass, but he slipped and fell into the mud. His jersey got dirty. This made the boy very sad. He went home and washed the mud out of his jersey. The jersey was wet, so he went outside and tied a rope between two trees. *Draw a line between the two trees you drew on the board.* The boy hung the jersey on the line so it would dry. *Tape the T-shirt on the line between the trees.*

Picture:

This is the picture that will help you remember 3 x 3 = 9. Whenever you see 3 x 3, you will see two trees. When you see those two trees, you will remember the line running between the trees. Line rhymes with nine. You will remember the answer even faster if you see the jersey with the number 9 on it. Show picture of the two trees with the line between them. *(Large Flash Card 3 x 3)* **Remember, 3 x 3 = 9 or tree x tree = line.**

Activities:

❏ Have the students color the picture for the multiplication fact 3 x 3 on *Coloring Page 9* located on page 185. *[Activity 17, Page 134]*

❏ Have students act out the story. Two students stand up to pretend they are trees. Have each 'tree' hold the end of a rope or string. Another student pretends to be the boy who gets his football jersey dirty. Use shirt or paper jersey. Then have the student hang the jersey from the string. Have other students take turns as the actors. *[Activity 1, Page 133]*

❏ Choose an activity which best suits your class from the "Teaching Activities" section. (Pages 133-138)

Evaluate

Quiz the students over the multiplication facts learned so far.

Student Book

There was a boy who loved to play football with his friends. His parents knew how much he loved football, so they gave him a football jersey to wear. The number on the back was the number of his favorite professional football player. It was the number nine.

One day he was playing football with his friends. He was trying to catch a pass, but he slipped and fell in the mud. His jersey got dirty. This made the boy very sad. He went home and washed the mud out of his jersey. The jersey was wet, so he went outside and tied a rope between two trees. The boy hung the jersey on the line so it would dry.

Page 36

3 x 3 = 9

Tree x Tree = Line

Page 37

Materials:
❑ Large Flash Cards
❑ Coloring Page 3 x 4 (Page 185)
❑ Student Book (Pages 38 & 39)

FACT 3 x 4 = 12
Tree x Door = Elf

Introduce

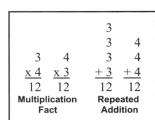

Tree   Door

Objective:
Students will learn the multiplication facts 3 x 4 = 12 and 4 x 3 =12.

Review:
Review the pictures two through nine and the multiplication facts learned so far.

Preparation:
Remind the students that 3 x 4 and 4 x 3 have the same answer. Write the multiplication facts 3 x 4 = 12 and 4 x 3 = 12, and the repeated addition facts on the board. Explain that 4 x 3 is four threes and 3 x 4 is three fours.

Introduction:
The next multiplication fact we will be learning is 3 x 4. Three times four is equal to twelve.

Close your eyes and picture an elf. Elf rhymes with twelve. This is the answer to the multiplication fact three times four and four times three. Do you know what an elf is? It is important you understand what an elf is, to understand the story for today. Explain if necessary.

What does an elf look like? Some answers might be pointed ears, a funny hat and shoes, etc. **Close your eyes and imagine what an elf would look like. Let me tell you a story about an elf who loved the forest.**

Present

Tree x Door = Elf

Story:
Once there was an elf. He loved the forest and enjoyed walking through the big tall trees. The elf decided he wanted to live in the forest because he liked it so much.

The elf came up with a great idea. He found a big tree, hollowed it out, and made his home inside. He put a door on his home. The elf loved living in the tree with a door.

Picture:
Close your eyes and picture the elf peeking out from behind his door in the tree. Show them the picture of 3 x 4 = 12. **Did the picture you saw look similar to this one? When you see the multiplication fact 3 x 4 or**

---

4 x 3, you will think of a tree and a door. When you think tree and door, you will remember a door on a tree. Instantly your mind will remember the elf peeking out from behind the door. The elf reminds you of the number 12.

What other picture do you remember that has an elf in it? 2 x 6 = 12. **2 x 6 and 3 x 4 have the same answer 12, but we use different pictures. How many pictures do you think you can put in your head?** A bunch, billions and billions.

Activities:

❑ Have the students color the picture for 3 x 4 on *Coloring Page 9* located on page 185. *[Activity 17, Page 134]*

❑ Choose an activity which best suits your class from the "Teaching Activities" section. (Pages 133-138)

Evaluate

Quiz the students over the multiplication facts learned so far. You may want to quiz the students using the large flash cards.

Student Book

Once there was an elf. He loved the forest and enjoyed walking through the big tall trees. The elf decided he wanted to live in the forest because he liked it so much.

The elf came up with a great idea. He found a big tree, hollowed it out, and made his home inside. He put a door on his home. The elf loved living in the tree with a door.

Page 38

3 x 4 = 12

Tree x Door = Elf

Page 39

Materials:
❑ Large Flash Cards
❑ Coloring Page 3 x 5 (Page 187)
❑ Student Book (Pages 40 & 41)

FACT 3 x 5 = 15
Tree x Hive = Lifting

Introduce

3	3	
	3	5
3 5	3 5	
x 5 x 3	+ 3 + 5	
15 15	15 15	
Multiplication Fact	Repeated Addition	

Tree   Hive

Objective:
Students will learn the multiplication facts 3 x 5 = 15 and 5 x 3 =15.

Review:
Review the pictures two through nine and the multiplication facts learned so far.

Preparation:
Write the multiplication facts 3 x 5 = 15 and 5 x 3 = 15 on the board and also the repeated addition facts. Discuss each.

Introduction:
Today you will learn a picture to help you remember 3 x 5 = 15 and 5 x 3 = 15. We will begin today by talking about trees.

Trees are made of wood and most are very strong. If you were strong like a tree, you might show off your muscles. Lift your arm and show your muscles. Do trees have arms? No, but limbs are like arms. **Close your eyes and imagine a tree with arms.**

To help you remember 3 x 5 = 15, we are going to picture a tree with arms. This tree is a kind tree which is nice to all animals.

Present

Tree x Hive = Lifting

Story:
Once there was a tree. He was a very kind tree who welcomed all animals. The birds, squirrels, and even bees liked playing in his limbs. The bees loved the tree so much they decided to build their hive in his branches.

One day a wind storm blew the hive out of the tree. The kind tree reached down with his arms and lifted the hive back into his branches. The hive was happy to be back in the tree.

Picture:
Show the students the picture of the tree lifting the hive. *(Large Flash Card 3 x 5)*

When you see a tree lifting the hive, you will remember the answer to the multiplication fact 3 x 5 = 15 and 5 x 3 = 15. When you see a tree

---

and a hive, you will remember the tree lifting the hive back into the tree. Lifting rhymes with fifteen.

Activities:

❏ Have the students color the picture for 3 x 5 on *Coloring Page 10* located on page 187. *[Activity 17, Page 134]*

❏ Have a student pantomime a multiplication fact story, while others in the class try to figure out which story it is. Do all of the facts learned so far. *[Activity 41, Page 136]*

❏ Choose an activity which best suits your class from the "Teaching Activities" section. (Pages 133-138)

Evaluate

Quiz the students over the multiplication facts learned so far.

Student Book

Once there was a tree. He was a very kind tree who welcomed all animals. The birds, squirrels, and even bees liked playing in his limbs. The bees loved the tree so much they decided to build their hive in his branches.

One day a wind storm blew the hive out of the tree. The kind tree reached down with his arms and lifted the hive back into his branches. The hive was happy to be back in the tree.

Page 40

$$3 \times 5 = 15$$

Tree x Hive = Lifting

Page 41

Materials:
- ❑ Large Flash Cards
- ❑ Coloring Page 3 x 6 (Page 187)
- ❑ Student Book (Pages 42 and 43)

FACT 3 x 6 = 18
Tree x Chicks = Aching

Introduce

```
          3
          3
          3
          3    6
   3   6  3    6
  x6  x3 +3   +6
  18   18 18   18
Multiplication  Repeated
    Fact        Addition
```

Tree   Chick

Objective:
Students will learn the multiplication facts 3 x 6 = 18 and 6 x 3 = 18.

Review:
Review the pictures two through nine and the multiplication facts learned so far.

Preparation:
Again, write the multiplication facts 3 x 6 and 6 x 3 and the repeated addition facts on the board. Discuss each.

Introduction:
Do you remember what it feels like to have a part of your body ache? Review the term ache from Lesson 16. (Toothache, headache, backache, etc.)

Stand up. I want you to walk around pretending you are chicks. Have the students lean over with their arms folded like wings. **Now, as you are walking around, I want you to pretend you are carrying a heavy tree. Not a little tree, but a large, heavy tree. How would your back feel?** It would start aching.

Present

Tree x Chicks =Aching

Story:
Once there were two chicks who lived on a farm. One day the wind blew so hard it knocked over a tree. The tree fell right in the middle of the yard where the chicks liked to play.

The chicks decided to move the tree out of the yard. They put the tree on their backs and carried the heavy tree out into a field. They were happy when they were finished, but their backs were aching.

Picture:
This is the picture you will remember when you think of the multiplication fact 3 x 6. When you see 3 x 6, you will picture a tree and chicks. When you picture a tree and chicks, you will automatically see chicks carrying a tree. This will remind you of their aching backs. So you will remember chicks (6) carrying a tree (3) and their backs are

---

aching (18). Use this picture to remember that 3 x 6 = 18. *(Large Flash Card 3 x 6)*

The students now have the pictures of all the numbers and the first twelve multiplication facts. They are more than one third of the way finished. Take some time and make sure the students 'see' each picture in their head.

Activities:
❑ Have the students color the picture for 3 x 6 on *Coloring Page 10* located on page 187. *[Activity 17, Page 134]*
❑ Have the students act out the story of the chicks and the heavy tree. *[Activity 1, Page 133]*
❑ Choose an activity which best suits your class from the "Teaching Activities" section. (Pages 133-138)

Evaluate

In pairs, have the students test each other by using the small flash cards. Quiz the students over the multiplication facts learned so far.

Student Book

Once there were two chicks who lived on a farm. One day the wind blew so hard it knocked over a tree. The tree fell right in the middle of the yard where the chicks liked to play.

The chicks decided to move the tree out of the yard. They put the tree on their backs and carried the heavy tree out into a field. They were happy when they were finished, but their backs were aching.

Page 42

3 x 6 = 18

Tree x Chicks = Aching

Page 43

Materials:
❏ Picture Quiz 2 (Page 142)

Review 2
Quiz on 2 x 2 through 3 x 6

Introduce

Objective:
Check student recall of the multiplication facts 2 x 2, 2 x 3, 2 x 4, 2 x 5, 2 x 6, 2 x 7, 2 x 8, 2 x 9, 3 x 3, 3 x 4, 3 x 5, and 3 x 6.

Preparation:
Have the students spread their desks apart, or move to where they are not tempted to share answers. Pass out a copy of *Picture Quiz 2* (Page 142) to each student.

Introduction:
Today you will be taking a quiz over the multiplication facts you have learned. This quiz is a picture quiz. I want you to draw the picture you see in your head that helps you remember each of the multiplication facts you have learned.

Present

At the top of the page, please write your name and the date.

Look at the upper left box. It says, "In this box, draw the picture for 2 x 2." When I say, "Begin," draw the picture you see in your mind for 2 x 2. Draw a picture in each of the boxes. If you don't remember one of the pictures, skip it and come back to it after you have drawn the rest of the pictures.

Take your time to draw each picture with detail. If you finish before I say stop, you may take out your crayons and color the pictures. You will have 10 minutes to complete the drawings.

Are there any questions? Answer basic questions.

You may begin. Check the time. Students have ten minutes to complete the quiz.

After ten minutes . . .

Stop. Collect and score the papers.

Tests

Picture Quiz 2

Picture Quiz 2

Name_____

Date _____ Score_____

In this box, draw the picture for **2 x 2**.	In this box, draw the picture for **2 x 3** (and 3 x 2).	In this box, draw the picture for **2 x 4** (and 4 x 2).
In this box, draw the picture for **2 x 5** (and 5 x 2).	In this box, draw the picture for **2 x 6** (and 6 x 2).	In this box, draw the picture for **2 x 7** (and 7 x 2).
In this box, draw the picture for **2 x 8** (and 8 x 2).	In this box, draw the picture for **2 x 9** (and 9 x 2).	In this box, draw the picture for **3 x 3**.
In this box, draw the picture for **3 x 4** (and 4 x 3).	In this box, draw the picture for **3 x 5** (and 5 x 3).	In this box, draw the picture for **3 x 6** (and 6 x 3).

Materials:
❑ Large Flash Cards
❑ Coloring Page 3 x 7 (Page 189)
❑ Student Book (Pages 44 & 45)
❑ Aluminum Can

FACT 3 x 7 = 21
Tree x Surfin' = Denty Sun

Introduce

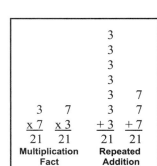

		3	
		3	
		3	
		3	
		3	7
3	7	3	7
x 7	x 3	+ 3	+ 7
21	21	21	21
Multiplication Fact		**Repeated Addition**	

Tree   Surfin

Present

Tree x Surfin' = Denty Sun

Objective:
Students will learn the multiplication facts 3 x 7 = 21 and 7 x 3 = 21.

Review:
Review the pictures two through nine and the multiplication facts learned so far.

Preparation:
Write the multiplication facts 3 x 7 = 21, 7 x 3 = 21, and the repeated addition fact on the board. Again, take the time to discuss what 3 x 7 and 7 x 3 represent.

Introduction:
For the next picture you will need to understand what a dent is. Who knows what a dent is? Lead a discussion about what a dent is. Describe a dent in a car, an aluminum can, etc. **If a car or a can had many dents in it, we would say it is denty. How many of you have seen a denty car?** Discuss the term 'denty' with the students. Have students come up to the front of the room and put dents in the aluminum can, making it a denty can.

Let's review the basic pictures for the multiplication fact 3 x 7 = 21. What is the picture for three? Tree. **What picture do you see for seven?** Surfin'. Show the pictures for each number.

Story:
A huge tree was tired of standing in the forest all day. He went down to the beach, rented a surfboard, and went surfing. The tree was having fun surfing when suddenly it crashed into the sun. The tree was so tall, he had reached all the way to the sun.

The tree hit the sun so hard it made dents in the sun. The sun became a denty sun.

Picture:
Close your eyes. Can you picture a tree bumping into the sun while riding on a surfboard? This is the picture you will use to remember the answer 21. Picture a surfin' (7) tree (3) making a denty sun. (21)

You might want to discuss with the students how this story and others are impossible, but they can still see the picture in their heads.

Show students the picture of the surfing tree bumping into the sun. *(Large Flash Card 3 x 7)*

Activities:

❑ Have the students color the 3 x 7 picture on *Coloring Page 11* located on page 189. *[Activity 17, Page 134]*
❑ Have the students act out the story of the tree surfing.
[Activity 1, Page 133]
❑ Choose an activity which best suits your class from the "Teaching Activities" section. (Pages 133-138)

Evaluate

Quiz the students over the multiplication facts learned so far.

Student Book

A huge tree was tired of standing in the forest all day. He went down to the beach, rented a surfboard, and went surfing. The tree was having fun surfing when suddenly it crashed into the sun. The tree was so tall, he had reached all the way to the sun. The tree hit the sun so hard it made dents in the sun. The sun became a denty sun.	**3 x 7 = 21**  **Tree x Surfin' = Denty Sun**
Page 44	*Page 45*

Materials:
- ❑ Large Flash Cards
- ❑ Coloring Page 3 x 8 (Page 189)
- ❑ Student Book (Pages 46 & 47)

FACT 3 x 8 = 24
Tree x Skate = Denty Floor

Introduce

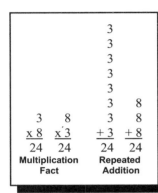

Multiplication Fact		Repeated Addition	
		3	
		3	
		3	
		3	
		3	
		3	8
3	8	3	8
x 8	x 3	+ 3	+ 8
24	24	24	24

Tree

Skate

Objective:
Students will learn the multiplication facts 3 x 8 = 24 and 8 x 3 = 24.

Review:
Review the pictures two through nine and the multiplication facts learned.

Preparation:
Write the multiplication facts 3 x 8 = 24, 8 x 3 = 24, and the repeated addition facts on the board. Discuss.

Introduction:
Do you remember the giant tree we talked about when you learned the multiplication fact 3 x 7 = 21? What happened when he tried to go surfing? The tree made a denty sun. **Well, this tree got into more trouble before he went back to the forest.**

Present

Tree x Skate = Denty Floor

Story:
Once there was a huge tree. This tree wanted to have some fun. He decided to go roller skating. He went to a skating rink and put on skates. The tree was having a great time until the owner came over to tell him to stop skating.

The owner said, "You are a very, very, heavy tree. I can see you are having a great time skating, but look what you are doing to the floor. You are making a denty floor! Please stop!"

Picture:
Can you imagine what a giant tree wearing roller skates would do to the floor of a skating rink? You are right. As the tree skated around, he would make big dents in the floor.

Students, please stand. Pretend you are a tree on roller skates. Imagine you are a very heavy tree putting on roller skates. Put your hands behind your back and pretend you are roller skating. Bang, bang, bang, your roller skates are denting the floor.

This is the picture I want you to remember. Close your eyes and see a giant tree skating. As he skates, his skates make big dents in the floor.

This picture will help you remember 3 x 8 = 24. Every time you see 3 x 8, you will remember a tree (3) on skates (8). When you see a tree on skates, you will remember the denty floor (24).

Activities:

❏ Have the students color the 3 x 8 picture on *Coloring Page 11* located on page 189. *[Activity 17, Page 134]*

❏ Choose an activity which best suits your class from the "Teaching Activities" section. (Pages 133-138)

Evaluate

Quiz the students over the multiplication facts learned so far.

Student Book

Once there was a huge tree. This tree wanted to have some fun. He decided to go roller skating. He went to a skating rink and put on skates. The tree was having a great time until the owner came over to tell him to stop skating.

The owner said, "You are a very, very, heavy tree. I can see you are having a great time skating, but look what you are doing to the floor. You are making a denty floor! Please stop!"

Page 46

3 x 8 = 24

Tree x Skate = Denty Floor

Page 47

Materials:
❑ Large Flash Cards
❑ Coloring Page 3 x 9 (Page 191)
❑ Student Book (Pages 48 & 49)

FACT 3 x 9 = 27
Tree x Sign = Denty Chef's Van

Introduce

```
        3
        3
        3
        3
        3
        3
        3       9
  3     9       3       9
 x 9   x 3     + 3     + 9
 27    27      27      27
Multiplication    Repeated
    Fact          Addition
```

Tree

Sign

Objective:
Students will learn the multiplication facts 3 x 9 = 27 and 9 x 3 = 27.

Review:
Review the pictures two through nine and the multiplication facts learned so far.

Preparation:
Write the multiplication facts 3 x 9 = 27, 9 x 3 = 27, and the repeated addition facts on the board. Discuss with your students what 3 x 9 and 9 x 3 represent.

Introduction:
Let us review a minute before we begin. Have a student come to the board and draw the picture he or she remembers for three and nine. Show the students the *Large Flash Card 3 x 9*.

For this picture, you will need to know what a chef is. A chef is the head cook at a restaurant. Do any of you know what type of hat a chef wears? Lead a discussion about chefs and what they do.

Let me tell you a story which goes with this picture.

Present

**Tree x Sign =
Denty Chef's Van**

Story:
A tree decided to have a party for its forest friends. He wanted to serve great food, so he called a chef who did his cooking in a special van. The chef said he would go to the forest and prepare the meal in his van.

The chef asked the tree how he would know which tree to go to since many of the trees in the forest look alike. The tree said he would be waving a sign.

The chef drove his van around the forest looking for a tree waving a sign. As he drove through the forest, he kept running into branches of other trees. These branches put small dents in his van. By the time the chef got to the tree who was waving the sign, his van was covered with dents. It was a denty chef's van.

Picture:
Close your eyes. Can you picture a tree waving a sign, trying to get a denty chef van to stop? This is the picture you will use to remember the answer, 27. Picture a tree (3) waving a sign (9) at a denty chef van. (27)

Activities:
❑ Have the students color the 3 x 9 picture on *Coloring Page 12* located on page 191. *[Activity 17, Page 134]*
❑ Choose an activity which best suits your class from the "Teaching Activities" section. (Pages 133-138)

Evaluate

Quiz the students over the multiplication facts learned so far. Use *Quick Quiz 3* located on page 146.

Student Book

A tree decided to have a party for its forest friends. He wanted to serve great food, so he called a chef who did his cooking in a special van. The chef said he would go to the forest and cook the meal in his van.

The chef asked the tree how he would know which tree to go to since many of the trees in the forest look alike. The tree said he would be waving a sign.

The chef drove his van around the forest looking for a tree waving a sign. As he drove through the forest, he kept running into branches of other trees. These branches put small dents in his van. By the time the chef got to the tree who was waving the sign, his van was covered with dents. It was a denty chef's van.

Page 48

3 x 9 = 27

Tree x Sign = Denty Chef's Van

Page 49

Materials:
❑ Large Flash Cards
❑ Coloring Page 4 x 4 (Page 191)
❑ Paper Crown
❑ Student Book (Pages 50 & 51)

FACT 4 x 4 = 16
Door x Door = Sick Queen

Introduce

```
        4
        4
  4     4
 x 4   + 4
 16     16

Multiplication  Repeated
    Fact        Addition
```

Door   Door

Objective:
Students will learn the multiplication fact 4 x 4 = 16.

Review:
Reviewing is the key to students remembering the multiplication facts. As you review the multiplication facts learned, have the students describe the pictures they see for each multiplication fact.

Preparation:
Write 4 x 4 = 16 on the board. Discuss with the students that 4 x 4 is actually a quick way of writing four fours, or 4 + 4 + 4 + 4.

Introduction:
Today we are going to start learning the fours. Show the *Large Flash Card* for four. **What multiplication facts do we already know that have a door in them?** Have students come to the front board and draw the images for 2 x 4 = 8 and 3 x 4 = 12.

You are going to learn a new picture today. It will help you remember 4 x 4 = 16. To understand this picture you need to know about revolving doors. Take a few minutes and discuss how a revolving door works.

Present

Door x Door =
Sick Queen

Story:
One evening, there was a party for a queen at a big hotel. The hotel had revolving doors.

When the queen got to the hotel, she was amazed to see the revolving doors. She had never seen such interesting doors. She pushed the doors and went around and around and around because it was so much fun. Soon she became dizzy and felt sick. She became a sick queen.

Picture:
Have the students stand up and pretend they are the queen going around in the revolving door. Let the students twirl until they are dizzy.

When you see 4 x 4 you will remember two doors, the revolving doors. When you remember the revolving doors, instantly, you will remember a sick queen or 16.

Show the *Large Flash Card* for 4 x 4 = 16. Point out the sick queen and the revolving doors. Discuss.

Activities:

❑ Have the students color the 4 x 4 picture on *Coloring Page 12* located on page 191. *[Activity 17, Page 134]*

❑ Have the students act out the queen using the revolving door. Let students wear the crown. *[Activity 11, Page 133]*

❑ Choose an activity which best suits your class from the "Teaching Activities" section. (Pages 133-138)

Evaluate

Quiz the students over the multiplication facts learned so far.

Student Book

One evening, there was a party for a queen at a big hotel. The hotel had revolving doors.

When the queen got to the hotel, she was amazed to see the revolving doors. She had never seen such interesting doors. She pushed the doors and went around and around and around because it was so much fun. Soon she became dizzy and felt sick. She became a sick queen.

Page 50

4 x 4 = 16

Door x Door = Sick Queen

Page 51

Materials:
❑ Large Flash Cards
❑ Coloring Page 4 x 5 (Page 193)
❑ Student Book (Pages 52 & 53)

FACT 4 x 5 = 20
Door x Hive = Honey

Introduce

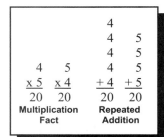

Door   Hive

Objective:
Students will learn the multiplication facts 4 x 5 = 20 and 5 x 4 = 20.

Review:
Review the pictures two through nine and the multiplication facts learned so far.

Preparation:
Write the multiplication facts 4 x 5 = 20, 5 x 4 = 20, and the repeated addition facts on the board and discuss.

Introduction:
Close your eyes and picture a hive with a door. If bees left the door of a hive open, what would come dripping out? Honey.

Here is a story that will help you remember 4 x 5 = 20 and 5 x 4= 20.

Present

Door x Hive = Honey

Story:
Bees work very hard and they are very proud of their bee hive. They leave their hive every day to find pollen to make honey.

One day, the bees left the door to the hive open by mistake. With the door open, out dripped much of the honey.

Picture:
Show the *Large Flash Card* for 4 x 5 = 20.

This picture will help you remember 5 x 4 = 20. Door and hive will remind you that when the door of the hive is left open, out drips the honey. The word honey rhymes with 20. Door times hive equals honey or 4 x 5 = 20.

Activities:
❑ Have a student pantomime a multiplication fact story while others in the class try to figure out which story it is. Do all of the facts learned so far. *[Activity 41, Page 136]*

❏ Have the students color the 4 x 5 picture on *Coloring Page 13* located on page 193. *[Activity 17, Page 134]*
❏ Choose an activity which best suits your class from the "Teaching Activities" section. (Pages 133-138)

Evaluate

Quiz the students over the multiplication facts learned.

Student Book

Bees work very hard and they are very proud of their bee hive. They leave their hive every day to find nectar to make honey.

One day, the bees left the door to the hive open by mistake. With the door open, out dripped much of the honey.

Page 52

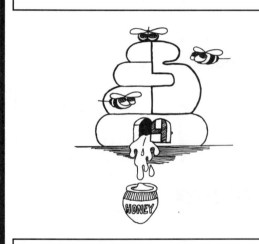

4 x 5 = 20

Door x Hive = Honey

Page 53

Materials:
- ❑ Large Flash Cards
- ❑ Coloring Page 4 x 6 (Page 193)
- ❑ Student Book (Pages 54 & 55)

FACT 4 x 6 = 24
Door x Chicks = Denty Floor

Introduce

```
              4
              4
              4   6
              4   6
      4   6   4   6
     x 6  x 4  + 4  + 6
      24   24   24   24
   Multiplication   Repeated
       Fact        Addition
```

Door   Chicks

Objective:
Students will learn the multiplication facts 4 x 6 = 24 and 6 x 4 =24.

Review:
Review the pictures two through nine and the multiplication facts learned.

Preparation:
Write the multiplication facts 4 x 6 = 24, 6 x 4 = 24, and the repeated addition facts on the board. Discuss each.

Introduction:
When you see the number four, what do you 'see' in your mind? Door.
What do you see when you think of the number six? Chicks.

Today you will learn a story about some chicks who get into trouble. This story will help you remember the multiplication fact 4 x 6 = 24.

Present

Door x Chicks =
Denty Floor

Story:
It was a very cold day on a farm. The ground was covered with snow and some of the chicks could not find any food. They became very hungry. While looking for food, they noticed the farmer had left the door of his house open. The chicks walked in. The floor had not been swept for a few days, so the chicks were able to find crumbs of food on the floor. When they pecked at the food, their beaks made tiny dents in the floor. The farmer now had a denty floor.

The farmer came into the house, gathered up the chicks, and took them to the barn and fed them. He was careful not to leave the door open again.

Picture:
This story will help you remember 4 x 6 = 24. When you see 4 x 6, you will remember a door and a chick. This will remind you of the chicks (6) coming through the door (4) and making a denty floor. (24)

What other multiplication fact has 24 (denty floor) as the answer?
3 x 8 = 24 **Remember the tree on skates made a denty floor also.**

Activities:
❑ Have the students color the 4 x 6 picture on *Coloring Page 13* located on page 193. *[Activity 17, Page 134]*
❑ Have students act out the story of the chicks coming through the door and pecking at the floor. *[Activity 1, Page 133]*
❑ Choose an activity which best suits your class from the "Teaching Activities" section. (Pages 133-138)

Evaluate

Use the large flash cards to quiz the students over the multiplication facts learned so far.

Student Book

It was a very cold day on a farm. The ground was covered with snow and some of the chicks could not find any food. They became very hungry. While looking for food, they noticed the farmer had left the door of his house open. The chicks walked in. The floor had not been swept for a few days, so the chicks were able to find crumbs of food on the floor. When they pecked at the food, their beaks made tiny dents in the floor. The farmer now had a denty floor.

The farmer came into the house, gathered up the chicks, and took them to the barn and fed them. He was careful not to leave the door open again.

Page 54

4 x 6 = 24

Door x Chick = Denty Floor

Page 55

Materials:
- ❑ Large Flash Cards
- ❑ Coloring Page 4 x 7 (Page 195)
- ❑ Aluminum Pie Plate
- ❑ Student Book (Pages 56 & 57)

FACT 4 x 7 = 28
Door x Surfin' = Denty Plate

Introduce

```
            4
            4
            4
            4    7
            4    7
   4    7   4    7
  x 7  x 4  +4   +7
  ----  ----  ----  ----
  28   28   28   28
Multiplication   Repeated
     Fact        Addition
```

Door   Surfin'

Objective:
Students will learn the multiplication facts 4 x 7 = 28 and 7 x 4 = 28.

Review:
Review the pictures two through nine and the multiplication facts.

Preparation:
Write the multiplication facts 4 x 7 = 28, 7 x 4 = 28, and the repeated addition facts on the board and discuss.

Introduction:
Today, you will learn that four times seven is equal to twenty-eight. Remember, 4 x 7 and 7 x 4 have the same answer.

To help us remember 4 x 7 = 28, we use a strange picture and story. Strange pictures are like funny pictures. They are very easy to remember.

Present

Door x Surfin' =
Denty Plate

Story:
There was a door who was a waiter. He worked at a pizza place on the waterfront. The door's job was to deliver pizzas to people on boats. To do this, he hopped on a surfboard and surfed to the boats.

The door had a favorite metal plate he used to carry the pizzas. Sometimes, the plate would bang into the side of the boat and get a dent in it. After the door had delivered pizzas for a few weeks, the plate was very denty.

Picture:
Close your eyes and picture what a door would look like carrying a pizza and riding a surfboard.

Everyone stand up. Close your eyes and imagine you are the door delivering a pizza. Imagine you have two pizzas, one balanced on each hand. It's hard to balance them both, isn't it?

Now imagine smashing into a boat while riding a surfboard. Have the students act it out.

The next time you see the multiplication fact 4 x 7, you will picture a door surfing. When you picture a surfing door, you will remember the waiter making a denty plate. (28) 4 x 7 = 28. Show the *Large Flash Card* for 4 x 7 = 28.

Activities:

❏ Have the students color the 4 x 7 picture on *Coloring Page 14* located on page 195. *[Activity 17, Page 134]*

❏ Have students act out the door surfing with a plate. The students hold the aluminum pie plate as they pretend to surf. *[Activity 1, Page 133]*

❏ Choose an activity which best suits your class from the "Teaching Activities" section. (Pages 133-138)

Evaluate

Quiz the students over the multiplication facts learned so far.

Student Book

There was a door who was a waiter. He worked at a pizza place on the waterfront. The door's job was to deliver pizzas to people on boats. To do this, he hopped on a surfboard and surfed to the boats.

The door had a favorite metal plate he used to carry the pizzas. Sometimes, the plate would bang into the side of the boat and get a dent in it. After the door had delivered pizzas for a few weeks, the plate was very denty.

4 x 7 = 28

Door x Surfin' = Denty Plate

Page 56   *Page 57*

Materials:
❑ Large Flash Cards
❑ Coloring Page 4 x 8 (Page 195)
❑ Student Book (Pages 58 & 59)

FACT 4 x 8 = 32
Door x Skate = Dirty U

Introduce

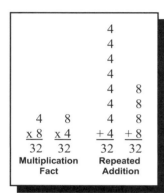

```
              4
              4
              4
              4
              4   8
              4   8
    4   8     4   8
   x 8  x 4  +4  +8
   32   32    32   32
  Multiplication  Repeated
      Fact       Addition
```

Door   Skate

Objective:
Students will learn the multiplication facts 4 x 8 = 32 and 8 x 4 = 32.

Review:
Review the pictures two through nine and the multiplication facts learned so far.

Preparation:
Write the multiplication facts 4 x 8 = 32, 8 x 4 = 32, and the repeated addition facts on the board, discussing each.

Introduction:
Do you remember when the door was a waiter? In the last lesson, what did he do? Delivered pizza and ran into ships, making a denty plate.

The door also did other things. The next story about the door will help you remember the multiplication fact 4 x 8 = 32.

Present

Shoe x Door =
Dirty U

Story:
Once there was a door who loved to roller skate. He would put on his roller skates and skate all around town.

One day, the door was skating by an old pile of dirty wood when he had a great idea. He built a huge ramp shaped like a U. The door called his ramp the dirty U because it was made of dirty wood. He loved skating up and down the sides of the U. He learned how to do all kinds of tricks on the dirty U.

Picture:
Close your eyes and picture the door skating on roller skates. Now picture him zipping up and down the sides of the dirty U ramp. Show the students the *Large Flash Card 4 x 8*. Discuss.

This is the picture that will remind you that 4 x 8 = 32. When you see the multiplication fact 4 x 8 you will remember a door on skates. When you

picture a door on skates, you will instantly remember him skating on the dirty U ramp (32).

Activities:
❑ Have the students color the 4 x 8 picture on *Coloring Page 14* located on page 195. *[Activity 17, Page 134]*
❑ Have the students act out the story of the skating door. *[Activity 1, Page 133]*
❑ Choose an activity which best suits your class from the "Teaching Activities" section. (Pages 133-138)

Evaluate

Give the students a written evaluation of the multiplication facts learned so far.

Student Book

Once there was a door who loved to roller skate. He would put on his roller skates and skate all around town. One day, the door was skating by an old pile of dirty wood when he had a great idea. He built a huge ramp shaped like a U. The door called his ramp the dirty U because it was made of dirty wood. He loved skating up and down the sides of the U. He learned how to do all kinds of tricks on the dirty U.	**4 x 8 = 32** 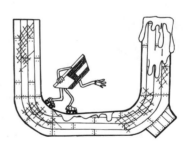 **Door x Skate = Dirty U**
Page 58	*Page 59*

Materials:
❑ Large Flash Cards
❑ Coloring Page 4 x 9 (Page 197)
❑ Student Book (Pages 60 & 61)

FACT 4 x 9 = 36
Door x Sign = Dirty Sticks

Introduce

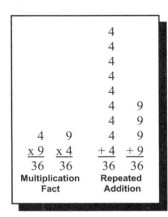

		4	
		4	
		4	
		4	
		4	
		4	9
		4	9
4	9	4	9
x 9	x 4	+ 4	+ 9
36	36	36	36
Multiplication Fact		Repeated Addition	

Door

Sign

Objective:
Students will learn the multiplication facts 4 x 9 = 36 and 9 x 4 = 36.

Review:
Review the pictures two through nine and the multiplication facts learned so far.

Preparation:
Write the multiplication facts 4 x 9 = 36, 9 x 4 = 36, and the repeated addition facts on the board, discussing each.

Introduction:
What picture do you see for the number 4? Door. **What picture do you see for 9?** Sign. **Close your eyes and picture a sign. Now imagine a sign with a door that opens and closes.** Show the class the Large Flash Card 4 x 9.

Here is a story to help you remember 4 x 9 = 36.

Present

Door x Sign = Dirty Sticks

Story:
Once there was a sign near a lumber mill. A lumber mill is a factory where trees are made into boards. The trees coming from the forest were often very dirty. Sometimes, as the lumber trucks rumbled by the sign, dirty sticks would fall out.

The sign liked to keep the street clean, so it would reach down and pick up the dirty sticks. The sign would put the sticks behind its secret door. It knew people would want clean sticks to burn in their fireplaces. The sign would keep the dirty sticks behind the door until it rained. Then it would hold the sticks out in the rain to clean them. It would stack the clean sticks near the road where people could pick them up to use in their fireplaces.

The sign would then wait for more dirty sticks to put behind the secret door.

Picture:

Close your eyes and picture the sign with the secret door. Now see the sign reaching down and picking up the dirty sticks.

This is the picture that will remind you 4 x 9 = 36. When you see the multiplication fact 4 x 9 you will remember a secret door on a sign. When you picture a door on a sign, you will instantly remember the sign picking up the dirty sticks. 4 x 9 = 36

Activities:

❑ Have the students color the 4 x 9 picture on *Coloring Page 15* located on page 197. *[Activity 17, Page 134]*

❑ Choose an activity which best suits your class from the "Teaching Activities" section (Pages 133-138)

Evaluate

Quiz the students over the multiplication facts learned so far. Use *Quick Quiz 4* located on page 146.

Student Book

Once there was a sign near a lumber mill. A lumber mill is a factory where trees are made into boards. The trees coming from the forest were often very dirty. Sometimes, as the lumber trucks rumbled by the sign, dirty sticks would fall out.

The sign liked to keep the street clean, so it would reach down and pick up the dirty sticks. The sign would put the sticks behind its secret door. It knew people would want clean sticks to burn in their fireplaces. The sign would keep the dirty sticks behind the door until it rained. Then it would hold the sticks out in the rain to clean them. It would stack the clean sticks near the road where people could pick them up to use in their fireplaces.

The sign would then wait for more dirty sticks to put behind the secret door.

Page 60

4 x 9 = 36

Door x Sign = Dirty Sticks

Page 61

Materials:
- ☐ Large Flash Cards
- ☐ Coloring Page 5 x 5 (Page 197)
- ☐ Student Book (Pages 62 & 63)

FACT 5 x 5 = 25
Hive x Hive = Denty Dive

Introduce

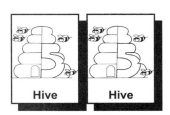

```
        5
        5
        5
    5   5
  x 5  + 5
  ----  ----
   25   25
```

Multiplication   Repeated
Fact   Addition

Hive   Hive

Objective:
Students will learn the multiplication fact 5 x 5 = 25.

Review:
Reviewing is the key to students remembering the multiplication facts. Review the multiplication facts learned.

Preparation:
Write 5 x 5 = 25 on the board. Discuss with the students that 5 x 5 is actually a shorthand way of writing five fives or 5 + 5 + 5 + 5 + 5.

Introduction:
The next multiplication fact we will learn is 5 x 5. Five times five equals twenty-five.

What is the image for the number five? Hive. **Who will come to the board and draw it for the class?** Have one student come forward and draw a hive.

Today I will tell you a story and show you a picture that will help you remember 5 x 5 = 25. Be sure to remember a hive represents the number five.

Present

Hive x Hive =
Denty Dive

Story:
One very hot day, two bee hives went to a swimming pool to cool off. They had a great time. They splashed in the water and chased each other around. They even dove off the diving board, but there was a problem. They were so heavy, they made dents in the diving board when they bounced on it. The hives named their dive, denty dive, because of the denty diving board.

Picture:
Close your eyes and picture two hives bouncing on a diving board, making it denty. Show the students the *Large Flash Card* for 5 x 5. **This is the picture that will help you remember 5 x 5 = 25. When you see 5 x 5 you will remember two hives. The two hives, 5 x 5, made a denty dive. (25)** Discuss until the students fully understand and can remember the picture.

Again, remember that the key to remembering the multiplication facts is repetition.

Activities:
❑ Have the students color the 5 x 5 picture on *Coloring Page 15* located on page 197. *[Activity 17, Page 134]*
❑ Choose an activity which best suits your class from the "Teaching Activities" section (Pages 133-138)

Evaluate

Quiz the students over the multiplication facts learned. Emphasize the fives.

Student Book

One very hot day, two bee hives went to a swimming pool to cool off. They had a great time. They splashed in the water and chased each other around. They even dove off the diving board, but there was a problem. They were so heavy, they made dents in the diving board when they bounced on it. The hives named their dive, denty dive, because of the denty diving board.

Page 62

5 x 5 = 25

Hive x Hive = Denty Dive

Page 63

Materials:
❑ Large Flash Cards
❑ Coloring Page 5 x 6 (Page 199)
❑ Student Book (Pages 64 & 65)

FACT 5 x 6 = 30
Hive x Chicks = Dirty

Introduce

$$
\begin{array}{cc}
5 & \\
5 & 6 \\
5 & 6 \\
5 & 6 \\
5 & 6 \\
+5 & +6 \\
\hline
30 & 30
\end{array}
$$

$$
\begin{array}{cc}
5 & 6 \\
\times 6 & \times 5 \\
\hline
30 & 30
\end{array}
$$

Multiplication   Repeated
Fact   Addition

Hive   Chick

Present

Hive x Chick =
Dirty

Objective:
Students will learn the multiplication facts 5 x 6 = 30 and 6 x 5 = 30.

Review:
Review the pictures two through nine and the multiplication facts learned so far.

Preparation:
Write the multiplication facts 5 x 6 = 30 and 6 x 5 = 30 on the board. Also write the repeated addition facts on the board. Discuss each.

Introduction:
The next multiplication fact is 5 x 6. Five times six equals thirty.

Here is a story to help you remember 5 x 6 = 30. It is a story about some chicks and a hive that wanted to have some fun.

Story:
One day some chicks were lonely. They asked a hive if it wanted to go to a nearby farm and play. The hive said, "Sure, sounds like fun!" So off they went to the farm.

They had a great time. The hive's favorite place was the pig pen. The hive and the chicks loved playing in the mud. They even rode the dirty pig and threw mud all over each other. Oh, what a great day they had playing in the mud and getting dirty!

Picture:
Close your eyes and imagine a hive and some chicks riding on a pig and getting dirty. Imagine them covered with dirt. They got really dirty, but the hive and the chick had the best time playing in the pig pen! Remember the chicks and a hive are dirty. If you remember this picture you will remember 6 x 5 = 30.

Show the students the picture of the chicks and the hive getting dirty at the farm. *(Large Flash Card 6 x 5)*

Activities:
❏ Have the students color the 5 x 6 picture on *Coloring Page 16* located on page 199. *[Activity 17, Page 134]*
❏ Have the students act out the story of the chicks and the hive. *[Activity 1, Page 133]*
❏ Choose an activity which best suits your class from the "Teaching Activities" section (Pages 133-138)

Evaluate

In pairs, have the students test each other by using the small flash cards. Quiz the students over the multiplication facts learned up to this point.

Student Book

One day some chicks were lonely. They asked a hive if it wanted to go to a nearby farm and play. The hive said, "Sure, sounds like fun!" So off they went to the farm.

They had a great time. The hive's favorite place was the pig pen. The hive and the chicks loved playing in the mud. They even rode the dirty pig and threw mud all over each other. Oh, what a great day they had playing in the mud and getting dirty!

Page 64

5 x 6 = 30

Hive x Chicks = Dirty

Page 65

Materials:
❏ Large Flash Cards
❏ Coloring Page 5 x 7 (Page 199)
❏ Student Book (Pages 66 & 67)

FACT 5 x 7 = 35
Hive x Surfin' = Dirty Dive

Introduce

```
          5
          5
          5   7
          5   7
          5   7
    5  7  5   7
   x 7 x 5 + 5  + 7
   35  35  35   35
Multiplication  Repeated
    Fact        Addition
```

Hive   Surfin'

Objective:
Students will learn the multiplication facts 5 x 7 = 35 and 7 x 5 = 35.

Review:
Review the pictures two through nine and the multiplication facts learned so far.

Preparation:
Write the multiplication facts 5 x 7 = 35 and 7 x 5 = 35 on the board. Again, write the repeated addition facts on the board and discuss.

Introduction:
Do you remember the story about the chicks and the hive? After the hive visited the farm and got dirty, he went surfing at the beach and got even dirtier.

Some beaches are sandy, some are rocky, and others are muddy. Guess which beach the hive visited? Yes, this story takes place on a muddy beach.

This story will help you remember 7 x 5 = 35.

Present

Hive x Surfin' =
Dirty Dive

Story:
A hive went to the beach. He was afraid of getting hurt on the rocks and the sandy beaches were too hot for his feet, so he went to a muddy beach.

The hive had a funny way of surfing at the muddy beach. He would surf up to the beach and dive right into the mud. Soon he was very dirty! The hive loved doing the dirty dives.

Picture:
This picture will help you remember the multiplication fact 5 x 7 = 35. When you see 5 x 7, you will remember a hive surfing. It is a picture of the surfing hive doing a dirty dive. The hive (5) went surfing (7) and did a dirty dive (35).

Activities:

❑ Have the students color the 5 x 7 picture on *Coloring Page 16* located on page 199. *[Activity 17, Page 134]*

❑ Have the students act out the story of the surfing hive.
[Activity 1, Page 133]

❑ Choose an activity which best suits your class from the "Teaching Activities" section. (Pages 133-138)

Evaluate

Allow students time to review independently with their flash cards. Then, quiz the students over the multiplication facts learned so far.

Student Book

5 x 7 = 35

Hive x Surfin' = Dirty Dive

A hive went to the beach. He was afraid of getting hurt on the rocks and the sandy beaches were too hot for his feet, so he went to a muddy beach.

The hive had a funny way of surfing at the muddy beach. He would surf up to the beach and dive right into the mud. Soon he was very dirty! The hive loved doing the dirty dives.

Page 66

Page 67

Materials:
❑ Picture Quiz 3 (Page 143)

Review 3
Quiz on 3 x 7 through 5 x 7

Introduce

Objective:
Check student recall on the multiplication facts 3 x 7, 3 x 8, 3 x 9, 4 x 4, 4 x 5, 4 x 6, 4 x 7, 4 x 8, 4 x 9, 5 x 5, 5 x 6, and 5 x 7.

Review:
None

Preparation:
Have the students spread their desks apart or move to where they are not tempted to share answers. Pass out a copy of *Picture Quiz 3* to each student.

Introduction:
Today you will be taking a quiz over the multiplication facts you have learned so far. This quiz is a picture quiz. You are to draw the picture you see in your head that helps you remember each of the multiplication facts you have learned.

Present

At the top of the page, please write your name and the date.

Look at the upper left box. It says, "In this box, draw the picture for 3 x 7." When I say, "Begin," draw the picture you see in your mind for 3 x 7. Draw a picture in each of the boxes. If you don't remember one of the pictures, skip it and come back to it after you have drawn the rest of the pictures.

Take your time to draw each picture with detail. If you finish before I say stop, you may take out your crayons and color the pictures. You will have 10 minutes to complete the drawings.

Are there any questions? Answer basic questions.

You may begin. Check the time. Students have ten minutes to complete the quiz.

After ten minutes . . .

Stop. Collect and score the papers.

Tests   **Picture Quiz 3**

Picture Quiz 3

Name_____

Date _____ Score_____

In this box, draw the picture for **3 x 7** (and 7 x 3).	In this box, draw the picture for **3 x 8** (and 8 x 3).	In this box, draw the picture for **3 x 9** (and 9 x 3).
In this box, draw the picture for **4 x 4**.	In this box, draw the picture for **4 x 5** (and 5 x 4).	In this box, draw the picture for **4 x 6** (and 6 x 4).
In this box, draw the picture for **4 x 7** (and 7 x 4).	In this box, draw the picture for **4 x 8** (and 8 x 4).	In this box, draw the picture for **4 x 9** (and 9 x 4).
In this box, draw the picture for **5 x 5**.	In this box, draw the picture for **5 x 6** (and 6 x 5).	In this box, draw the picture for **5 x 7** (and 7 x 5).

Memorize in Minutes: The Times Tables
http://www.multiplication.com
143

Materials:
❑ Large Flash Cards
❑ Coloring Page 5 x 8 (Page 201)
❑ Student Book (Pages 68 & 69)

FACT 5 x 8 = 40
Hive x Skate = Fort E

Introduce

```
            5
            5
            5
            5    8
            5    8
            5    8
   5    8   5    8
  x 8   x 5  +5   +8
  ---   ---  ---  ---
  40    40   40   40
Multiplication  Repeated
    Fact        Addition
```

Hive

Skate

Objective:
Students will learn the multiplication facts 5 x 8 = 40 and 8 x 5 = 40.

Review:
Review the pictures two through nine and the multiplication facts.

Preparation:
Write the multiplication facts 5 x 8 = 40 and 8 x 5= 40 on the board, along with the repeated addition facts on the board.

Introduction:
Before you learn another hive story, let me tell you about some people who live in a fort. Take some time with your students and explain forts. **Forts were used for protection in the early days. They often had logs surrounding them to provide protection against attack. Many forts served as trading posts on the American frontier. They had large gates that could be opened and closed.** After you feel students have a good understanding of a fort, continue with the lesson.

Once, a group of people decided to build fort that looked like the forts built by early pioneers. The first fort was Fort A and the second was Fort B. Can you guess the names of the other forts? Fort C, Fort D, and Fort E. **Fort E was the fifth fort built to look like a fort of long ago. The people who lived in Fort E dressed like pioneers and sometimes even acted like the people did long ago. During the summer, Fort E was a popular place for tourists.**

Present

Story:
Fort E was a fort built to look like forts of long ago. The people who lived in Fort E dressed and acted like pioneers. Visitors would come from all around to visit Fort E.

One summer day, a hive decided to skate over to Fort E. He put on his skates and went racing down the street. The people in Fort E saw the hive zooming toward them on skates and were afraid. They worried the bees from the hive would scare the visitors away, so they quickly shut the big

**Hive x Skate =
Fort E**

gates to the fort. The hive tried to stop, but he couldn't. He smashed right into the side of Fort E.

Picture:

This is the picture you will use to remind you that 5 x 8 = 40. The hive (5) on skates (8) is smashing into Fort E (40).

Activities:

❑ Have the students color the 5 x 8 picture on *Coloring Page 17* located on page 201. *[Activity 17, Page 134]*
❑ Have students act out the story of the skating hive.
[Activity 1, Page 133]
❑ Building a model of Fort E is a fun activity. *[Activity 36, Page 136]*
❑ Choose an activity which best suits your class from the "Teaching Activities" section (Pages 133-138)

Evaluate

Give the students a written evaluation of the multiplication facts learned so far.

Student Book

Fort E was a fort built to look like forts of long ago. The people who lived in Fort E dressed and acted like pioneers. Visitors would come from all around to visit Fort E. One summer day, a hive decided to skate over to Fort E. He put on his skates and went racing down the street. The people in Fort E saw the hive zooming toward them on skates and were afraid. They worried the bees from the hive would scare the visitors away, so they quickly shut the big gates to the fort. The hive tried to stop, but he couldn't. He smashed right into the side of Fort E.	**5 x 8 = 40**  **Hive x Skate = Fort E**
Page 68	*Page 69*

Materials:
❑ Large Flash Cards
❑ Coloring Page 5 x 9 (Page 201)
❑ Student Book (Pages 70 & 71)

FACT 5 x 9 = 45
Hive x Sign = Fort E Dive

Introduce

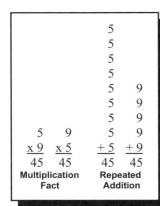

		5	
		5	
		5	
		5	
		5	9
		5	9
		5	9
5	9	5	9
x 9	x 5	+ 5	+ 9
45	45	45	45

Multiplication   Repeated
Fact   Addition

Hive

Sign

Objective:
Students will learn the multiplication facts 5 x 9 = 45 and 9 x 5 = 45.

Review:
Review the pictures two through nine and the multiplication facts learned so far.

Preparation:
Write the multiplication facts 5 x 9 = 45 and 9 x 5 = 45 and the repeated addition facts on the board. Discuss each.

Introduction:
This is your last picture with a hive in it. This picture will help you remember 5 x 9 = 45 and 9 x 5 = 45.

As you remember, the hive was trying to visit Fort E. When the people at Fort E shut the gate and the hive smashed into the side of Fort E, he was very sad. He took off his skates and was about to leave the fort when he had another idea.

Present

Hive x Sign =
Fort E Dive

Story:
The hive really wanted to get into Fort E. He thought and thought about it and came up with a great idea. He went to a nearby sign. He jumped into the air and onto the face of the sign. The sign bent back and then sprang forward, throwing the hive up into the air and over the high wall of Fort E. He ended up diving into Fort E.

The people in Fort E soon found out the bees in the hive were friendly. The people were very impressed with the hive's dive into the fort.

Picture:
Show the students the picture of the hive being catapulted off the sign into Fort E. **Close your eyes and picture what happened. This picture will help you remember 5 x 9 = 45. The hive (5) used a sign (9) to do a Fort E dive (45).**

Activities:
❏ Have the students color the 5 x 9 picture on *Coloring Page 17* located on page 201. *[Activity 17, Page 134]*
❏ Choose an activity which best suits your class from the "Teaching Activities" section. (Pages 133-138)

Evaluate

Give the students a written evaluation on the multiplication facts learned so far. Use *Quick Quiz 5* located on page 147.

Student Book

5 x 9 = 45

The hive really wanted to get into Fort E. He thought and thought about it and came up with a great idea. He went to a nearby sign. He jumped into the air and onto the face of the sign. The sign bent back and then sprang forward, throwing the hive up into the air and over the high wall of Fort E. He ended up diving into Fort E.

The people in Fort E soon found out the bees in the hive were friendly. The people were very impressed with the hive's dive into the fort.

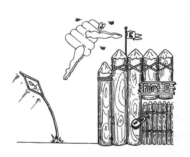

Hive x Sign = Fort E Dive

Page 70   *Page 71*

Materials:
❑ Large Flash Cards
❑ Coloring Page 6 x 6 (Page 203)
❑ Student Book (Pages 72 and 73)

FACT 6 x 6 = 36
Chicks x Chicks = Dirty Chicks

Introduce

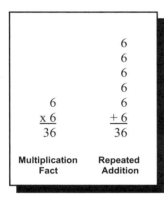

| Multiplication Fact | Repeated Addition |

Chick   Chick

Objective:
Students will learn the multiplication fact 6 x 6 = 36.

Review:
Remember to review the multiplication facts learned.

Preparation:
Write the multiplication fact 6 x 6 = 36 and the repeated addition fact on the board and discuss each.

Introduction:
The next multiplication fact you will learn is 6 x 6 = 36.

Here is a story to help you remember 6 x 6 = 36.

Present

Chicks x Chicks =
Dirty Chicks

Story:
It was a warm, sunny day. Some chicks were playing on the farm. They were scratching at the dry dirt trying to act like big chickens. It was very dusty. The chicks got very dirty. The other animals on the farm saw the chicks and said, "Chicks, chicks, dirty chicks!"

Picture:
This picture will help you remember 6 x 6 = 36. Whenever you see 6 x 6, you will think of chicks and chicks. When chicks (6) get together with other chicks (6), you have dirty chicks (36).

Say, "chicks, chicks, dirty chicks." It will help you remember 6 x 6 = 36. Repeat it many times over and over in your head or out loud. Chicks, chicks, dirty chicks.

Show the students the picture of the dirty chicks. *(Large Flash Card 6 x 6)*

Activities:

❑ Have the students color the 6 x 6 picture on *Coloring Page 18* located on page 203. *[Activity 17, Page 134]*

❑ Have the students in the class act out the story and repeat the phrase, "Chicks, chicks, dirty chicks."*[Activity 1, Page 133]*

❑ Choose an activity which best suits your class from the "Teaching Activities" section. (Pages 133-138)

Evaluate

Quiz the students over the multiplication facts learned so far. Again, have each student meet with a partner and practice with their flash cards.

Student Book

It was a warm, sunny day. Some chicks were playing on the farm. They were scratching at the dry dirt trying to act like big chickens. It was very dusty. The chicks got very dirty. The other animals on the farm saw the chicks and said, "Chicks, chicks, dirty chicks!"

Page 72

6 x 6 = 36

Chicks x Chicks = Dirty Chicks

Page 73

Materials:
❑ Large Flash Cards
❑ Coloring Page 6 x 7 (Page 203)
❑ Student Book (Pages 74 and 75)

FACT 6 x 7 = 42
Chicks x Surfin' = Fort E Zoo

Introduce

```
            6
            6    7
            6    7
            6    7
            6    7
      6  7  6    7
     x7  x6 +6  +7
     42  42  42  42
  Multiplication  Repeated
      Fact        Addition
```

Chick

Surfin'

Objective:
Students will learn the multiplication facts 6 x 7 = 42 and 7 x 6 = 42.

Review:
Review the pictures two through nine and the multiplication facts learned so far.

Preparation:
Write the multiplication facts 6 x 7 = 42, 7 x 6 = 42, and the repeated addition facts on the board and discuss.

Introduction:
Today you will learn that six times seven is equal to forty-two. Remember that 6 x 7 and 7 x 6 have the same answer.

Today you will learn a picture and a story that will help you remember that 6 x 7 = 42.

Present

**Chicks x Surfin' =
Fort E Zoo**

Story:
The chicks were very excited because they were going to take a school field trip to the zoo. This was no ordinary zoo. It was the zoo at Fort E. The Fort E Zoo was far away, near the ocean, so the chicks took a bus.

The bus ride was long, but soon the chicks could see the ocean and they knew they were getting close. The bus driver stopped at the beach and let the chicks get out to stretch their legs. While walking on the beach, the chicks saw a surfboard. They all thought of the same idea together, "Let's surf the rest of the way to the Fort E Zoo!" They hopped on the surfboard and surfed over to the fort. The chicks had a great day at the Fort E Zoo.

Picture:
Using this picture, you will always remember 6 x 7 = 42. Just remember that chicks (6) went surfin' (7) to the Fort E Zoo. (42)

Activities:

❑ Have the students color the 6 x 7 picture on *Coloring Page 18* located on page 203. *[Activity 17, Page 134]*

❑ Choose an activity which best suits your class from the "Teaching Activities" section. (Pages 133-138)

Evaluate

Quiz the students over the multiplication facts learned so far.

Student Book

The chicks were very excited because they were going to take a school field trip to the zoo. This was no ordinary zoo. It was the zoo at Fort E. The Fort E Zoo was far away, near the ocean, so the chicks took a bus.

The bus ride was long, but soon the chicks could see the ocean and they knew they were getting close. The bus driver stopped at the beach and let the chicks get out to stretch their legs. While walking on the beach, the chicks saw a surfboard. They all thought of the same idea together, "Let's surf the rest of the way to the Fort E Zoo!" They hopped on the surfboard and surfed over to the fort. The chicks had a great day at the Fort E Zoo.

Page 74

6 x 7 = 42

Chicks x Surfin' = Fort E Zoo

Page 75

Materials:
❏ Large Flash Cards
❏ Coloring Page 6 x 8 (Page 205)
❏ Cupcakes & frosting
❏ Student Book (Pages 76 and 77)

FACT 6 x 8 = 48
Chicks x Skate = Fort E Cake

Introduce

```
            6
            6
            6   8
            6   8
            6   8
            6   8
    6   8   6   8
  x 8  x 6  + 6  + 8
  ───  ───  ───  ───
   48   48   48   48
Multiplication  Repeated
     Fact       Addition
```

Chick

Skate

Objective:
Students will learn the multiplication facts 6 x 8 = 48 and 8 x 6 = 48.

Review:
Review the pictures two through nine and the multiplication facts learned so far.

Preparation:
Write the multiplication facts 6 x 8 = 48 and 8 x 6 = 48 on the board. Also write the repeated addition facts on the board and discuss.

Introduction:
Today you will learn another story and picture involving Fort E that will help you remember 6 x 8 = 48.

This is a funny story that tells what the chicks did when they got back from Fort E.

Present

Chicks x Skate = Fort E Cake

Story:
The chicks enjoyed their visit to Fort E. When they got home, the chicks baked a cake and decorated it to look like Fort E. It even had a flag with an E on it.

One of the chicks thought of a fun way to eat the Fort E Cake. The other chicks jumped up and down when they heard the idea. The chick told them to put on their skates, race by the cake, and take a bite with their beaks.

What happened next was funny. Some of the chicks were not very good skaters, so they skated right into the side of the cake. Splat!

Picture:
Close your eyes and picture chicks skating by a cake that looks like Fort E. Can you see the chicks trying to grab some cake with their beaks and smashing right into the side of the cake? This funny picture will remind you of the answer to the multiplication fact 6 x 8 = 48. The chicks (6) on skates (8) ate the Fort E cake. (48)

Activities:

❑ Have the students color the 6 x 8 picture on *Coloring Page 19* located on age 205. *[Activity 17, Page 134]*

❑ Bring in cupcakes to share with the students. You may have the students decorate them of bring them to class pre-decorated. The students can pretend to be chicks on skates and eat the cupcakes with their 'beaks.'

❑ Choose an activity which best suits your class from the "Teaching Activities" section. (Pages 133-138)

Evaluate

Quiz the students over the multiplication facts learned so far.

Student Book

6 x 8 = 48

The chicks enjoyed their visit to Fort E. When they got home, the chicks baked a cake and decorated it to look like Fort E. It even had a flag with an E on it.

One of the chicks thought of a fun way to eat the Fort E Cake. The other chicks jumped up and down when they heard the idea. The chick told them to put on their skates, race by the cake, and take a bite with their beaks.

What happened next was funny. Some of the chicks were not very good skaters, so they skated right into the side of the cake. Splat!

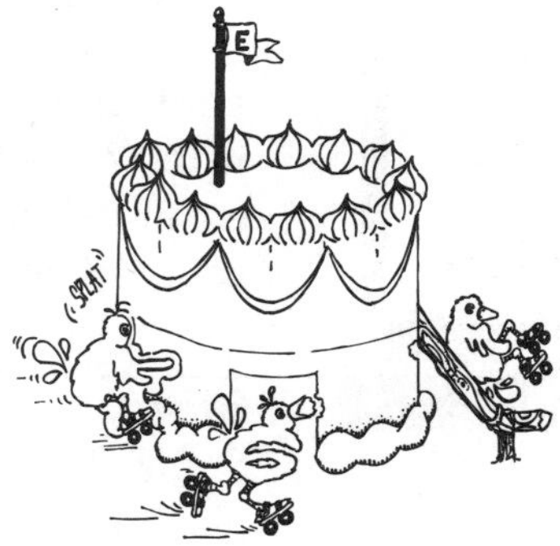

Chicks x Skate = Fort E Cake

Page 76   *Page 77*

Materials:
❑ Large Flash Cards
❑ Coloring Page 6 x 9 (Page 205)
❑ Fishing pole
❑ Gummy worms & apple
❑ Student Book (Pages 78 and 79)

FACT 6 x 9 = 54
Chicks x Sign = Fishing with Core

Introduce

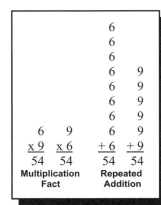

```
              6
              6
              6
              6    9
              6    9
              6    9
              6    9
    6    9    6    9
   x 9   x 6  + 6  + 9
   ────  ──── ──── ────
    54    54   54   54
Multiplication   Repeated
    Fact         Addition
```

Chick   **Sign**

Objective:
Students will learn the multiplication facts 6 x 9 = 54 and 9 x 6 = 54.

Review:
Review the pictures two through nine and the multiplication facts learned so far.

Preparation:
Write the multiplication facts 6 x 9 = 54 and 9 x 6 = 54 on the board. Also, write the repeated addition facts on the board and discuss.

Introduction:
This is the last picture to remember with chicks in it.

How many of you like apples? When you finish eating the apple, what is left? The apple core. **Can you imagine going fishing with an apple core? The chicks did. Fishing with an apple core will help you remember that 6 x 9 = 54.**

Present

**Chicks x Sign =
Fishing with Core**

Story:
Some chicks had a great idea for catching tasty worms. They dreamed up a plan to go fishing for worms. The chicks knew worms liked apples. So, they found a fishing pole and attached an old apple core to the end of the fishing line. Then, they climbed to the top of a sign so they could not be seen by the worms and lowered the apple core to the ground. Yum, the chicks caught some big, juicy worms!

Picture:
Isn't this a funny story? Close your eyes and picture chicks sitting on a sign fishing with an apple core. This picture is what will help you remember that 6 x 9 = 54. Just remember that chicks (6) on a sign (9) went fishing with a core (54).

Activities:

❑ Have the students color the 6 x 9 picture on *Coloring Page 19* located on page 205. *[Activity 17, Page 134]*
❑ Have the students act out the multiplication fact with a fishing pole, apple

---

core, and gummy worms. When most of the students have had a chance to act it out, have the gummy worms for a treat. You many also choose to use the gummy worms for a reward for those students who can remember the multiplication facts. *[Activity 1, Page 133]*

❑ Choose an activity which best suits your class from the "Teaching Activities" section. (Pages 133-138)

Evaluate

Use *Quick Quiz 6* on page 147 to quiz the students over the multiplication facts learned so far.

Student Book

Some chicks had a great idea for catching tasty worms. They dreamed up a plan to go fishing for worms. The chicks knew worms liked apples. So, they found a fishing pole and attached an old apple core to the end of the fishing line. Then, they climbed to the top of a sign so they could not be seen by the worms and lowered the apple core to the ground. Yum, the chicks caught some big, juicy worms!	**6 x 9 = 54** **Chicks x Sign = Fishing with Core**
Page 78	*Page 79*

Materials:
- ❏ Large Flash Cards
- ❏ Coloring Page 7 x 7 (Page 207)
- ❏ Student Book (Pages 80 and 81)
- ❏ Roll of twine
- ❏ Book of world records

FACT 7 x 7 = 49
Surfin' x Surfin' = Fort E Twine

Introduce

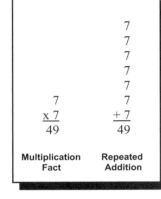

$$\begin{array}{r} 7 \\ x\,7 \\ \hline 49 \end{array} \qquad \begin{array}{r} 7 \\ 7 \\ 7 \\ 7 \\ 7 \\ 7 \\ +7 \\ \hline 49 \end{array}$$

Multiplication   Repeated
Fact   Addition

Surfin'   Surfin'

Objective:
Students will learn the multiplication fact 7 x 7 = 49.

Review:
Review the multiplication facts learned so far.

Preparation:
Write the multiplication fact 7 x 7 = 49 and the repeated addition fact on the board and discuss each.

Introduction:
The next multiplication fact we will learn is 7 x 7. Seven times seven equals forty-nine.

This is the last story about Fort E.

Before I tell you a story that will help you remember 7 x 7 = 49, you must know what twine is. Twine is like string, but stronger. It is made of string twisted together. Show the students a sample of a ball of twine, or have them make twine by twisting two pieces of string together.

Also, show students a book of world records. Read a small portion of the book so they understand what can be found in the book. If you do not have a book of world records, explain what the book is and why people want to be in it.

Present

Surfin' x Surfin' =
Fort E Twine

Story:
The people who lived in Fort E decided to make the world's largest ball of twine. They collected twine for many years and wound it into a ball. The ball of twine became bigger and bigger. After a few years, it was almost as big as the fort. It was the biggest ball of twine in the world.

The people of the fort had a problem. The ball was so big, they could not move around. The ball was too big to roll out the gate. The people did not want to unroll the twine, because then it wouldn't be the biggest ball of twine in the world. They finally decided to move out of Fort E and leave the twine there.

The ball of twine saved their lives. Soon after they moved out, two giant waves came crashing down on Fort E and destroyed the fort and the twine.

Picture:
This picture will help you remember that 7 x 7 = 49. When you see two sevens, you will remember two surfs. Surfs are waves without a person surfing. **When you see the two surfs (7) in your mind you will instantly remember them crashing down on the Fort E twine (49).**

Activities:
❑ Have the students color the 7 x 7 picture on *Coloring Page 20* located on page 207. *[Activity 17, Page 134]*
❑ Choose an activity which best suits your class from the "Teaching Activities" section. (Pages 133-138)

Evaluate

Quiz the students over the multiplication facts learned so far. Again, have students get with partners and quiz each other with flash cards.

Student Book

The people who lived in Fort E decided to make the world's largest ball of twine. They collected twine for many years and wound it into a ball. The ball of twine became bigger and bigger. After a few years, it was almost as big as the fort. It was the biggest ball of twine in the world.

The people of the fort had a problem. The ball was so big, they could not move around. The ball was too big to roll out the gate. The people did not want to unroll the twine, because then it wouldn't be the biggest ball of twine in the world. They finally decided to move out of Fort E and leave the twine there.

The ball of twine saved their lives. Soon after they moved out, two giant waves came crashing down on Fort E and destroyed the fort and the twine.

Page 80

7 x 7 = 49

Surfin' x Surfin' = Fort E Twine

Page 81

Materials:
❑ Large Flash Cards
❑ Coloring Page 7 x 8 (Page 207)
❑ Student Book (Pages 82 and 83)

FACT 7 x 8 = 56
Surfin' x Skate = Fishing for Sticks

Introduce

```
        7
        7   8
        7   8
        7   8
        7   8
        7   8
  7  8  7   8
 x 8 x 7 +7  +8
 56  56  56  56
Multiplication  Repeated
     Fact       Addition
```

Surfin'

Skate

Objective:
Students will learn the multiplication facts 7 x 8 = 56 and 8 x 7 = 56.

Review:
Review the pictures two through nine and the multiplication facts learned so far.

Preparation:
Write the multiplication facts 7 x 8 = 56 and 8 x 7 = 56 on the board. Also write the repeated addition facts on the board and discuss.

Introduction:
Today you will learn another picture. It will help you remember that 7 x 8 = 56.

First, we will review. When I say seven, what do you picture in your mind? Surfin'. **When I say eight, what picture do you see?** Skate. **This is a story about a surfing skate.** Show students the picture of the surfing skate on the *Large Flash Card 7 x 8.*

Present

Surfin' x Skate =
Fishing for Sticks

Story:
There was a roller skate who always wanted to learn how to surf. One day, it went to the beach and rented a surfboard. After some instruction, the skate learned how to surf.

It surfed all day and was having so much fun it did not want to stop. Near the end of the day, the skate started getting cold. It wanted to get warm but did not want to stop surfing. It came up with an idea. The roller skate borrowed a fishing pole from a man on the beach. As it surfed along, the skate would snag sticks with the hook. When it got to the beach, it took the sticks off the hook, put them in a pile, and went surfing again. Soon the skate had enough wood to build a fire and keep warm.

Picture:
What are some things in this story that could not really happen? Skates can't fish, it is hard to fish from a surf board, and the sticks would be too wet

---

to start a fire. Remind them that their brain can make up pictures that could not be true.

This story will help you remember the answer to multiplication fact 7 x 8 = 56. When you think 7 x 8, you will remember a surfing (7) skate (8) fishing for sticks. (56)

Activities:
❑ Have the students color the 7 x 8 picture on *Coloring Page 20* located on page 207. *[Activity 17, Page 134]*
❑ Choose an activity which best suits your class from the "Teaching Activities" section. (Pages 133-138)

Evaluate

Quiz the students over the multiplication facts learned so far.

Student Book

There was a roller skate who always wanted to learn how to surf. One day, it went to the beach and rented a surfboard. After some instruction, the skate learned how to surf.

It surfed all day and was having so much fun it did not want to stop. Near the end of the day, the skate started getting cold. It wanted to get warm but did not want to stop surfing. It came up with an idea. The roller skate borrowed a fishing pole from a man on the beach. As it surfed along, the skate would snag sticks with the hook. When it got to the beach, it took the sticks off the hook, put them in a pile, and went surfing again. Soon the skate had enough wood to build a fire and keep warm.

Page 82

7 x 8 = 56

Surfin' x Skate = Fishing for Sticks

Page 83

Materials:
❑ Large Flash Cards
❑ Coloring Page 7 x 9 (Page 209)
❑ Student Book (Pages 84 and 85)

FACT 7 x 9 = 63
Surfin' x Sign = Sticky Bee

Introduce

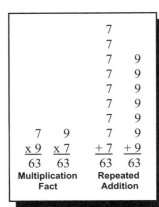

		7	
		7	
		7	9
		7	9
		7	9
		7	9
		7	9
7	9	7	9
x 9	x 7	+ 7	+ 9
63	63	63	63

Multiplication Fact   Repeated Addition

Surfin'

Sign

Objective:
Students will learn the multiplication facts 7 x 9 = 63 and 9 x 7 =63.

Review:
Review the pictures two through nine and the previous multiplication facts.

Preparation:
Write the multiplication facts 7 x 9 = 63 and 9 x 7 = 63 on the board. Also write the repeated addition facts on the board and discuss.

Introduction:
This is the last picture about surfing. This picture will help you remember 7 x 9 = 63.

This multiplication fact is 7 x 9. What do you think the sign is going to be doing? Surfing.

Present

Surfin' x Sign =
Sticky Bee

Story:
The sign saw all of its friends had learned to surf. It decided to learn to surf also. After a few lessons, the sign really liked surfing.

Something interesting happened to the sign one day. A bee, covered with sticky honey, was just buzzing along enjoying the warm summer day when... thud! The bee flew into the sign. Neither were hurt, but the sticky bee was stuck to the sign. The sign pulled and pulled at the bee and finally pulled the bee off.

The bee thanked the sign for helping him and flew away.

Picture:
This picture will help you remember 7 x 9 = 63. When you see 7 x 9, you will think of a surfing sign. The instant you see a surfing sign (9) you will remember the sign running into the sticky bee. (63)

Activities:
❏ Have the students color the 7 x 9 picture on *Coloring Page 21* located on page 209. *[Activity 17, Page 134]*
❏ Choose an activity which best suits your class from the "Teaching Activities" section. (Pages 133-138)

Evaluate

Use *Quick Quiz 7* on page 148 to quiz the students over the multiplication facts.

Student Book

The sign saw all of its friends had learned to surf. It decided to learn to surf also. After a few lessons, the sign really liked surfing.
 	
    Something interesting happened to the sign one day. A bee, covered with sticky honey, was just buzzing along enjoying the warm summer day when... thud! The bee flew into the sign. Neither were hurt, but the sticky bee was stuck to the sign. The sign pulled and pulled at the bee and finally pulled the bee off.
 	
    The bee thanked the sign for helping him and flew away.
	7 x 9 = 63
	
	**Surfin' x Sign =
	Sticky Bee**

Page 84	*Page 85*

Materials:
❑ Large Flash Cards
❑ Coloring Page 8 x 8 (Page 209)
❑ Student Book (Pages 86 and 87)

FACT 8 x 8 = 64
Skate x Skate = Sticky Floor

Introduce

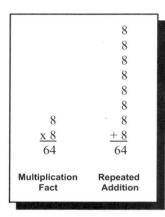

	8
	8
	8
	8
	8
	8
8	8
x 8	+ 8
64	64

Multiplication Fact   **Repeated Addition**

Skate   Skate

Objective:
Students will learn the multiplication fact 8 x 8 = 64.

Review:
Remember, reviewing is the key to students remembering the multiplication facts. Review the multiplication facts learned so far.

Preparation:
Write the multiplication fact 8 x 8 = 64 and the repeated addition fact on the board and discuss each.

Introduction:
The next multiplication fact we will learn is 8 x 8 = 64. Eight times eight equals sixty-four.

Present

Skate x Skate =
Sticky Floor

Story:
Two skaters went to a skating rink. They put on their skates and started skating. After only a few seconds, they stopped moving. They didn't know what was wrong. They looked down at the floor and were shocked. The floor was covered with sticky, gooey gum. Their skates were stuck to the sticky floor.

Picture:
When you see 8 x 8, you will picture two skates. When you think of two skaters, what pops into your head? Sticky floor. **Remember, two skaters (8) are trying to skate on a sticky floor. (64)**

Show the students the two children whose roller skates are sticking to the floor. *(Large Flash Card 8 x 8)*

Activities:
❑ Have the students color the 8 x 8 picture on *Coloring Page 21* located on page 209. *[Activity 17, Page 134]*
❑ Students enjoy acting out this story. Have the students **pretend** there is sticky gum on the floor. *[Activity 1, Page 133]*
❑ Choose an activity which best suits your class from the "Teaching Activities" section. (Pages 133-138)

Evaluate

Quiz the students over the multiplication facts learned so far. Again, have students use practice the multiplication facts with a partner.

Student Book

Two skaters went to a skating rink. They put on their skates and started skating. After only a few seconds, they stopped moving. They didn't know what was wrong. They looked down at the floor and were shocked. The floor was covered with sticky, gooey gum. Their skates were stuck to the sticky floor.

Page 86

8 x 8 = 64

Skate x Skate = Sticky Floor

Page 87

Materials:
- Large Flash Cards
- Coloring Page 8 x 9 (Page 211)
- Student Book (Pages 88 and 89)

FACT 8 x 9 = 72
Skate x Sign = 72 MPH

Introduce

```
        8
        8   9
        8   9
        8   9
        8   9
        8   9
        8   9
  8   9   8   9
 x 9  x 8  +8  +9
 72  72   72   72
```
Multiplication   Repeated
    Fact   Addition

Skate   Sign

Objective:
Students will learn the multiplication facts 8 x 9 = 72 and 9 x 8 = 72.

Review:
Review the pictures two through nine and the multiplication facts learned so far.

Preparation:
Write the multiplication facts 8 x 9 = 72 and 9 x 8 = 72 on the board. Also write the repeated addition facts on the board and discuss.

Introduction:
This is the last picture about skating. This picture will help you remember that 8 x 9 = 72.

This multiplication fact is 8 x 9. What do you think the sign is going to be doing? Skating.

Present

Skate x Sign =
72 MPH

Story:
Once there was a sign who was a really fast skater. This sign was special. The speed it was skating would show up on its face. If the sign skated 10 miles per hour, a 10 showed on its face.

One day the sign decided to skate as fast as it could. It found a deserted sidewalk and started skating. The sign skated faster and faster until it was skating 72 miles per hour.

Picture:
Why do you think the sign was able to go so fast? Thin, long legs. **If you were a policeman would you give the sign a speeding ticket?**

This picture will help you remember that 8 x 9 = 72. When you see 8 x 9, you will think of a skating (8) sign (9). The instant you 'see' a skating sign you will remember the sign with a 72 on his face.

Activities:
❑ Have the students color the 8 x 9 picture on *Coloring Page 22* located on page 211. *[Activity 17, Page 134]*
❑ Choose an activity which best suits your class from the "Teaching Activities" section. (Pages 133-138)

Quiz the students over the multiplication facts learned using *Quick Quiz 8* on page 148.

Student Book

8 x 9 = 72

Once there was a sign who was a really fast skater. This sign was special. The speed it was skating would show up on its face. If the sign skated 10 miles per hour, a 10 showed on its face.

One day the sign decided to skate as fast as it could. It found a deserted sidewalk and started skating. The sign skated faster and faster until it was skating 72 miles per hour.

Skate x Sign = 72 MPH

Page 88   *Page 89*

Materials:
- ❏ Large Flash Cards
- ❏ Coloring Page 9 x 9 (Page 211)
- ❏ Straws and construction paper
- ❏ Student Book (Pages 90 and 91)

FACT 9 x 9 = 81
Sign x Sign = Ate a Ton

Introduce

```
            9
            9
            9
            9
            9
            9
            9
    9       9
  x 9     + 9
   81      81
```

Multiplication Fact	Repeated Addition

Sign'   Sign

Objective:
Students will learn the multiplication fact 9 x 9 = 81.

Review:
Review the multiplication facts learned so far.

Preparation:
Write the multiplication fact 9 x 9 = 81 and the repeated addition fact on the board and discuss each.

Introduction:
The next multiplication fact we will learn is 9 x 9. Nine times nine equals eighty-one. This is the last multiplication fact you are going to learn.

For this story and picture you need to know what a ton is. What is a ton? A ton is 2000 pounds. A truck load full of dirt might weigh a ton. Discuss.

If the average student in our class weighs 50 pounds, how many students will it take to equal a ton? It may help the students to work with a partner. Share with them that two students have a combined weight of 100 pounds. The answer would be 40 students.

This story is about a man who ate and ate.

Present

Sign x Sign =
Ate a Ton

Story:
There once was a very large man. He was a giant man. The more he ate, the bigger he grew. After many years, he was so big his silverware would not fit into his hands. He started using road signs instead of spoons. He would sit down to a meal with a sign in each hand and shovel the food in. He could eat a ton of food at a meal.

Picture:
This story will remind you that 9 x 9 = 81. When you see 9 x 9 you will remember two signs. As soon as you remember the two signs, the picture of the man using two signs to eat will appear in your head. You

will remember a man using two signs (9 x 9) who ate a ton (81).

Activities:

❑ Have the students color the 9 x 9 picture on *Coloring Page 22* located on page 211. *[Activity 17, Page 134]*

❑ Students have fun acting this story out. Students can make signs out of straws and construction paper and pretend to eat a ton. Popcorn is a fun food for students to eat with the pretend signs. *[Activity 1, Page 133]*

❑ Choose an activity which best suits your class from the "Teaching Activities" section. (Pages 133-138)

Evaluate

The students have now learned all the basic multiplication facts. Use *Quick Quiz 9a or 9b* on page 149 to make sure they know all the facts. Remember to quiz the students at least once a week for the next few months. Use the *Review Quizzes* on pages 152 and 153.

Student Book

There once was a very large man. He was a giant man. The more he ate, the bigger he grew. After many years, he was so big his silverware would not fit into his hands. He started using road signs instead of spoons. He would sit down to a meal with a sign in each hand and shovel the food in. He could eat a ton of food at a meal.

Page 90

$$9 \times 9 = 81$$

**Sign x Sign =
Ate a Ton**

Page 91

Materials:
❑ Picture Quiz 4 (Page 144)

Review 4
Quiz on 5 x 8 through 9 x 9

Introduce

Objective:
Check student recall on the multiplication facts 5 x 8, 5 x 9, 6 x 6, 6 x 7, 6 x 8, 6 x 9, 7 x 7, 7 x 8, 7 x 9, 8 x 8, 8 x 9, and 9 x 9.

Review:
None

Preparation:
Have the students spread their desks apart or move to where they are not tempted to share answers. Pass out a copy of *Picture Quiz 4* to each student.

Introduction:
Today you will be taking a quiz over the multiplication facts you have learned. This quiz is a picture quiz. I want you to draw the picture you see in your head that helps you remember each of the multiplication facts you have learned so far.

Present

At the top of the page, please write your name and the date.

Look at the upper left box. It says, "In this box, draw the picture for 5 x 8." When I say, "Begin," draw the picture you see in your mind for 5 x 8. Draw a picture in each of the boxes. If you do not remember one of the pictures, skip it and come back to it after you have drawn the rest of the pictures.

Take your time to draw each picture with detail. If you finish before I say stop, you may take out your crayons and color the pictures. You will have ten minutes to complete the drawings.

Are there any questions? Answer basic questions.

You may begin. Check the time. Students have ten minutes to complete the quiz.

After ten minutes . . .

Stop. Collect and score the papers.

Tests
Picture Quiz 4

Picture Quiz 4

Name_____

Date _____ Score_____

In this box, draw the picture for **5 x 8** (and 8 x 5).	In this box, draw the picture for **5 x 9** (and 9 x 5).	In this box, draw the picture for **6 x 6**.
In this box, draw the picture for **6 x 7** (and 7 x 6).	In this box, draw the picture for **6 x 8** (and 8 x 6).	In this box, draw the picture for **6 x 9** (and 9 x 6).
In this box, draw the picture for **7 x 7**.	In this box, draw the picture for **7 x 8** (and 8 x 7).	In this box, draw the picture for **7 x 9** (and 9 x 7).
In this box, draw the picture for **8 x 8**.	In this box, draw the picture for **8 x 9** (and 9 x 8).	In this box, draw the picture for **9 x 9**.

144
Memorize in Minutes: The Times Tables
http://www.multiplication.com

Materials:
❑ Post Test (Page 150)
❑ Answer Key (Page 154)
❑ Student Record Chart
  (Page 221 and 222)

Post Test

Introduce

Objective:
The post-test is used to measure a student's progress. The post-test should be compared to the pre-test. This test will determine which facts need to be reviewed.

Preparation:
Pass out the post-test.

Have the students spread their desks apart or move to where they are not tempted to share answers. Pass out the tests. Have the students keep them face down until you say to begin.

Present

Today you will be taking a test of the basic multiplication facts. The purpose of this test is to see how much you have learned. This test is similar to the test you took before we started learning the multiplication facts. Do as many problems as you can. Try to do your best. When you are finished, please sit quietly until the time is up.

Are there any questions? Answer basic questions.

You may begin. Check the time. Students have six minutes to finish the test.

After six minutes. . .

Stop! Collect the papers.

Evaluate

Correct the tests using the answer guide on page 153.

Fill out the *Student Record Chart* located on pages 217 and 218. The facts are in order again. This time, the first fact (2 x 2) is number thirty-six. The problems snake backward to number one.

As you fill out the chart, you can compare the progress of each student. It is common for students to miss one or two due to careless mistakes. Scanning down the list, you can easily see which facts need to be reviewed. The goal is for all students to get all facts correct.

Post-Test   Student Record Chart

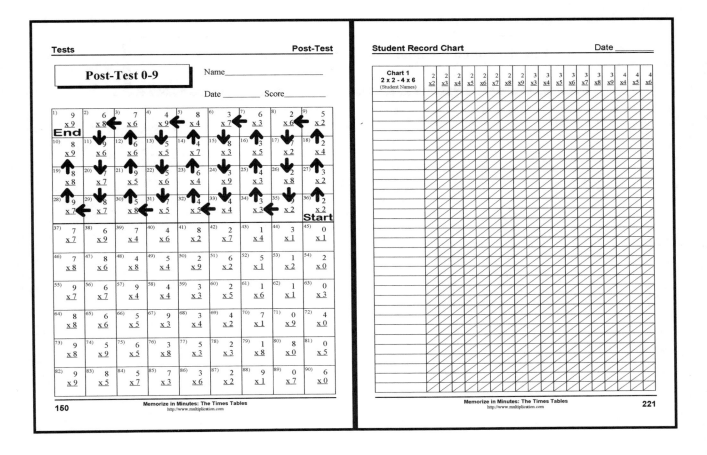

> **Teachers open the door, but you must enter by yourself.**
> Chinese Proverb

Chapter 3
Quick Lessons

Quick Lessons give you a quick overview of each lesson. Each lesson includes the story and the pictures for teaching each multiplication fact. After using the <u>Memorize in Minutes: The Times Tables</u> for a few years, many teachers teach from the Quick Lessons.

Materials:
❏ Large Flash Cards
❏ Coloring Page 2 x 2 (Page 177)
❏ Student Book (Pages 20 and 21)
❏ Lesson Plan 10, Page 32

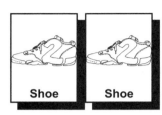

Shoe   Shoe

Shoe x Shoe =
Floor

FACT 2 x 2 = 4
Shoe x Shoe = Floor

Story:

A young boy received a new pair of shoes for his birthday. They were just the kind of shoes he had always wanted. When he put them on, he found they were too big. Even though they did not fit, he decided to wear them to school the next day. Sometimes, as he would walk along, he would step right out of them. He would look down at his feet and be in his socks. The shoes would be sitting on the floor. As you can imagine, this was very embarrassing for the boy.

Picture:

Picture two shoes (2 x 2) stuck to the floor. (4)

Materials:
❏ Large Flash Cards
❏ Coloring Page 2 x 3 (Page 177)
❏ Student Book (Pages 22 and 23)
❏ Lesson Plan 11, Page 34

Shoe   Tree

Shoe x Tree =
Sticks

FACT 2 x 3 = 6
Shoe x Tree = Sticks

Story:

There once were two young birds. They started building a nest because they were going to have their first babies. Building a nest turned out to be hard work. It takes many little sticks to build a nest and it seemed as if the nest would never get finished.

The birds were flying around looking for sticks when the mother bird saw an old shoe lying on the ground. The bird had a great idea. She picked up stick after stick and put them into the shoe. When the shoe was full, the two birds grabbed onto the shoe laces and flew back to the tree, carrying the shoe. When they got to the tree, they tied the shoe to a limb. By moving some of the sticks in the shoe, they quickly had a nest.

Picture:

Picture a shoe (2) in a tree (3) filled with sticks. (6)

Materials:
- ❏ Large Flash Cards
- ❏ Coloring Page 2 x 4 (Page 179)
- ❏ Student Book (Pages 24 and 25)
- ❏ Lesson Plan 12, Page 36

FACT 2 x 4 = 8
Shoe x Door = Plate

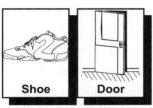

Shoe   Door

Shoe x Door =
Plate

Story:

There was an old lady who lived in a shoe. She had so many children she didn't know what to do. This lady loved pretty plates. Her children knew she liked pretty plates, so they would each buy her a plate for her birthday and many other holidays. After a while, she had so many plates they did not fit in her cupboards. She had to start stacking them everywhere around her house.

After many years, there were so many plates, when the front door was opened, out would roll plates.

Picture:

Picture a shoe (2) with a door (4) that has plates (8) rolling out of it.

Materials:
- ❏ Large Flash Cards
- ❏ Coloring Page 2 x 5 (Page 179)
- ❏ Student Book (Page 26 and 27)
- ❏ Lesson Plan 13, Page 38

FACT 2 x 5 = 10
Shoe x Hive = Pen

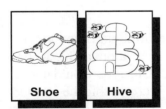

Shoe   Hive

Shoe x Hive =
Pen

Story:

Once upon a time there was a young bee hive who was very forgetful. His friends and parents would tell him things, but he would never remember them. To help him remember, he started to write himself notes, but he could never remember where he had put the notes.

Although he was forgetful, this hive was very clever. The hive bought a special pen that could be erased easily, and he started writing his notes on his shoes. Using his shoes and his special pen, the hive solved his problem.

Picture:

Picture a hive (5) writing on his shoe (2) with a pen. (10)

Materials:
❑ Large Flash Cards
❑ Coloring Page 2 x 6 (Page 181)
❑ Student Book (Pages 28 and 29)
❑ Lesson Plan 14, Page 40

FACT 2 x 6 = 12
Shoe x Chick = Elf

Story:

    A teacher decided to put on a winter play. A chick was chosen to be an elf, one of Santa's special helpers. He was so excited. When he went home that night, his mother made him an elf costume. She made little elf shoes and a little elf hat. He put them on and was very proud.

    During the play, the chick helped Santa deliver presents to good boys and girls. The chick had fun pretending he was an elf.

Picture:

Picture a chick (6) with shoes (2) that make him look like an elf. (12)

Materials:
❑ Large Flash Cards
❑ Coloring Page 2 x 7 (Page 181)
❑ Student Book (Pages 30 and 31)
❑ Lesson Plan 15, Page 42

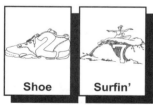

FACT 2 x 7 = 14
Shoe x Surfin' = Four Kings

Story:

    Four kings had been friends since they were children. If you looked at three of the kings, you would not see anything unusual about them, except they always wore their crowns. If you saw the fourth king, you would notice something strange. He had giant feet. His feet were so big he needed special shoes. The shoes had to be made just for him.

    Each year, the kings went on a vacation together. One year, they went to the beach. They watched the people surfing. It looked like fun, but they did not have surfboards.

    The king with the big feet had a funny idea. He thought they could all surf on his enormous shoes. So the four kings swam out into the water and three of the kings got on the shoulders of the king with the enormous shoes. When a wave came, the kings surfed to the beach on the enormous shoes. They had great fun surfing.

Picture:

Picture a four kings (14) surfing (7) on giant shoes. (2)

Materials:
- ❏ Large Flash Cards
- ❏ Coloring Page 2 x 8 (Page 183)
- ❏ Paper Crown
- ❏ Student Book (Pages 32 and 33)
- ❏ Lesson Plan 16, Page 44

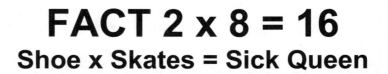

FACT 2 x 8 = 16
Shoe x Skates = Sick Queen

Shoe **Skate**

Shoe x Skate = Sick Queen

Story:

Once there was a silly queen. She loved to do things other queens would never think of doing. She wanted to learn how to roller skate. The queen went to a roller skating rink, rented roller skates, and sat down on a bench to take off her shoes. She put a skate on one foot and decided to stand up to see what it felt like to be on a skate. She lost her balance and before she knew what was happening, she started rolling. She rolled out onto the skating rink floor. She tried to stop, but started twirling and twirling and twirling. This made her feel sick. She was a sick queen.

Picture:

Picture a queen wearing one shoe (2) and one skate (8) who lost control and started spinning until she became a sick queen. (16)

Materials:
- ❏ Large Flash Cards
- ❏ Coloring Page 2 x 9 (Page 183)
- ❏ Yardstick
- ❏ Student Book (Pages 34 and 35)
- ❏ Lesson Plan 17, Page 46

FACT 2 x 9 = 18
Shoe x Sign = Aching

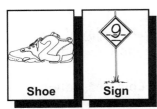

Shoe **Sign**

Shoe x Sign = Aching

Story:

Once there was a giant. He was really big. He was so big he couldn't go into buildings. It was lonely being a giant. Most people were afraid of him even though he was friendly.

One day he was so lonely he decided to go into the city. Most of the people ran away when they saw him. As he got near the center of town, he noticed some men with yellow hats working. The men did not see him. As he got closer, he could tell they were putting in a new sign. He walked up to the man holding onto the sign, tapped him on the shoulder, and said, "Hello." When the man saw the giant, he was so scared he dropped the sign and ran. The sign landed on the giant's shoe. OUCH! The giant's toe started aching!

Picture:

Picture a sign (9) falling on a giant's shoe (2) causing it to start aching. (18)

Materials:
- ❑ Large Flash Cards
- ❑ Coloring Page 3 x 3 (Page 185)
- ❑ T-shirt with 9 taped to it or Paper cut-out of a shirt
- ❑ Student Book (Pages 36 and 37)
- ❑ Lesson Plan 18, Page 48

FACT 3 x 3 = 9
Tree x Tree = Line

Story:
There was a boy who loved to play football with his friends. His parents knew how much he loved football, so they gave him a football jersey to wear. The number on the back was the number of his favorite professional football player. It was the number nine.

One day he was playing football with his friends. He was trying to catch a pass, but he slipped and fell in the mud. His jersey got dirty. This made the boy very sad. He went home and washed the mud out of his jersey. The jersey was wet, so he went outside and tied a rope between two trees. The boy hung the jersey on the line so it would dry.

Picture:
Picture two trees (3 & 3) with a line (9) between them holding a jersey.

Materials:
- ❑ Large Flash Cards
- ❑ Coloring Page 3 x 4 (Page 185)
- ❑ Student Book (Pages 38 and 39)
- ❑ Lesson Plan 19, Page 50

FACT 3 x 4 = 12
Tree x Door = Elf

Story:
Once there was an elf. He loved the forest and enjoyed walking through the big tall trees. The elf decided he wanted to live in the forest because he liked it so much.

The elf came up with a great idea. He found a big tree, hollowed it out, and made his home inside. He put a door on his home. The elf loved living in the tree with a door.

Picture:
Picture a door (4) on a tree (3) with an elf (12) peeking out.

Materials:
❑ Large Flash Cards
❑ Coloring Page 3 x 5 (Page 187)
❑ Student Book (Pages 40 and 41)
❑ Lesson Plan 20, Page 52

FACT 3 x 5 = 15
Tree x Hive = Lifting

Tree   Hive

Tree x Hive =
Lifting

Story:
 Once there was a tree. He was a very kind tree who welcomed all animals. The birds, squirrels, and even bees liked playing in his limbs. The bees loved the tree so much they decided to build their hive in his branches.
 One day a wind storm blew the hive out of the tree. The kind tree reached down with his arms and lifted the hive back into his branches. The hive was happy to be back in the tree.

Picture:
A hive fell out of the tree. Picture the tree (3) lifting (15) the hive (5) back into the tree.

Materials:
❑ Large Flash Cards
❑ Coloring Page 3 x 6 (Page 187)
❑ Student Book (Page 42 and 43)
❑ Lesson Plan 21, Page 54

FACT 3 x 6 = 18
Tree x Chick = Aching

Tree   Chick

Tree x Chick =
Aching

Story:
 Once there were two chicks who lived on a farm. One day the wind blew so hard it knocked over a tree. The tree fell right in the middle of the yard where the chicks liked to play.
 The chicks decided to move the tree out of the yard. They put the tree on their backs and carried the heavy tree out into a field. They were happy when they were finished, but their backs were aching.

Picture:
When chicks (6) carried a tree (3) they soon had aching (18) backs.

Materials:
❑ Large Flash Cards
❑ Coloring Page 3 x 7 (Page 189)
❑ Student Book (Pages 44 and 45)
❑ Lesson Plan 23, Page 58

FACT 3 x 7 = 21
Tree x Surfin' = Denty Sun

Tree x Surfin' =
Denty Sun

Story:
A huge tree was tired of standing in the forest all day. He went down to the beach, rented a surfboard, and went surfing. The tree was having fun surfing when suddenly it crashed into the sun. The tree was so tall, he had reached all the way to the sun.

The tree hit the sun so hard it made dents in the sun. The sun became a denty sun.

Picture:
Picture a tall tree (3) surfing. (7) It bumps into the sun making a denty sun. (21)

Materials:
❑ Large Flash Cards
❑ Coloring Page 3 x 8 (Page 189)
❑ Student Book (Pages 46 and 47)
❑ Lesson Plan 24, Page 60

FACT 3 x 8 = 24
Tree x Skate = Denty Floor

Tree x Skates =
Denty Floor

Story:
Once there was a huge tree. This tree wanted to have some fun. He decided to go roller skating. He went to a skating rink and put on skates. The tree was having a great time until the owner came over to tell him to stop skating.

The owner said, "You are a very, very, heavy tree. I can see you are having a great time skating, but look what you are doing to the floor. You are making a denty floor! Please stop!"

Picture:
Picture a tree (3) on skates (8) making a denty floor. (24)

Materials:
- ❑ Large Flash Cards
- ❑ Coloring Page 3 x 9 (Page 191)
- ❑ Student Book (Pages 48 and 49)
- ❑ Lesson Plan 25, Page 62

FACT 3 x 9 = 27
Tree x Sign = Denty Chef's Van

Tree   Sign

Tree x Sign =
Denty Chef's Van

Story:

A tree decided to have a party for its forest friends. He wanted to serve great food, so he called a chef who did his cooking in a special van. The chef said he would go to the forest and prepare the meal in his van.

The chef asked the tree how he would know which tree to go to since many of the trees in the forest look alike. The tree said he would be waving a sign.

The chef drove his van around the forest looking for a tree waving a sign. As he drove through the forest, he kept running into branches of other trees. These branches put small dents in his van. By the time the chef got to the tree who was waving the sign, his van was covered with dents. It was a denty chef's van.

Picture:

Picture a tree (3) waving a sign (9) at a denty chef's van. (27)

Materials:
- ❑ Large Flash Cards
- ❑ Coloring Page 4 x 4 (Page 191)
- ❑ Paper Crown
- ❑ Student Book (Pages 50 and 51)
- ❑ Lesson Plan 26, Page 64

FACT 4 x 4 = 16
Door x Door = Sick Queen

Door   Door

Door x Door =
Sick Queen

Story:

One evening, there was a party for a queen at a big hotel. The hotel had revolving doors.

When the queen got to the hotel, she was amazed to see the revolving doors. She had never seen such interesting doors. She pushed the doors and went around and around and around because it was so much fun. Soon she became dizzy and felt sick. She became a sick queen.

Picture:

Picture a two doors (4 & 4) revolving and making a sick queen. (16)

Materials:
❏ Large Flash Cards
❏ Coloring Page 4 x 5 (Page 193)
❏ Student Book (Pages 52 and 53)
❏ Lesson Plan 27, Page 66

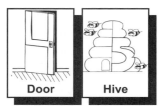

Door   **Hive**

**Door x Hive =
Honey**

FACT 4 x 5 = 20
Door x Hive = Honey

Story:
     Bees work very hard and they are very proud of their bee hive. They leave their hive every day to find pollen to make honey.
     One day, the bees left the door to the hive open by mistake. With the door open, out dripped much of the honey.

Picture:
Picture the door (4) on a hive (5) left open and honey (20) dripping from it.

Materials:
❏ Large Flash Cards
❏ Coloring Page 4 x 6 (Page 193)
❏ Student Book (Pages 54 and 55)
❏ Lesson Plan 28, Page 68

Door   **Chick**

**Door x Chicks =
Denty Floor**

FACT 4 x 6 = 24
Door x Chicks = Denty Floor

Story:
     It was a very cold day on a farm. The ground was covered with snow and some of the chicks could not find any food. They became very hungry. While looking for food, they noticed the farmer had left the door of his house open. The chicks walked in. The floor had not been swept for a few days, so the chicks were able to find crumbs of food on the floor. When they pecked at the food, their beaks made tiny dents in the floor. The farmer now had a denty floor.
     The farmer came into the house, gathered up the chicks, and took them to the barn and fed them. He was careful not to leave the door open again.

Picture:
Picture chicks (6) that came in an open door (4) and started pecking the floor making it a denty floor. (24)

Materials:
- ❏ Large Flash Cards
- ❏ Coloring Page 4 x 7 (Page 195)
- ❏ Aluminum Pie Plate
- ❏ Student Book (Pages 56 and 57)
- ❏ Lesson Plan 29, Page 70

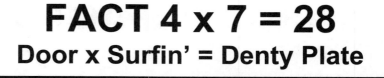

FACT 4 x 7 = 28
Door x Surfin' = Denty Plate

Door   Surfin'

Door x Surfin' =
Denty Plate

Story:

There was a door who was a waiter. He worked at a pizza place on the waterfront. The door's job was to deliver pizzas to people on boats. To do this, he hopped on a surfboard and surfed to the boats.

The door had a favorite metal plate he used to carry the pizzas. Sometimes, the plate would bang into the side of the boat and get a dent in it. After the door had delivered pizzas for a few weeks, the plate was very denty.

Picture:

Picture the door (4) who is surfing, (7) carrying a denty plate. (28)

Materials:
- ❏ Large Flash Cards
- ❏ Coloring Page 4 x 8 (Page 195)
- ❏ Student Book (Pages 58 and 59)
- ❏ Lesson Plan 30, Page 72

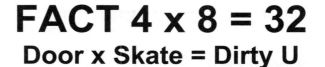

FACT 4 x 8 = 32
Door x Skate = Dirty U

Door   Skate

Door x Skate =
Dirty U

Story:

Once there was a door who loved to roller skate. He would put on his roller skates and skate all around town.

One day, the door was skating by an old pile of dirty wood when he had a great idea. He built a huge ramp shaped like a U. The door called his ramp the dirty U because it was made of dirty wood. He loved skating up and down the sides of the U. He learned how to do all kinds of tricks on the dirty U.

Picture:

Picture a door (4) on skates (8) skating on the dirty U (32) ramp.

Materials:
❑ Large Flash Cards
❑ Coloring Page 4 x 9 (Page 197)
❑ Student Book (Pages 60 and 61)
❑ Lesson Plan 31, Page 74

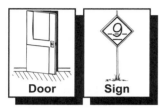

Door x Sign =
Dirty Sticks

FACT 4 x 9 = 36
Door x Sign = Dirty Sticks

Story:
 Once there was a sign near a lumber mill. A lumber mill is a factory where trees are made into boards. The trees coming from the forest were often very dirty. Sometimes, as the lumber trucks rumbled by the sign, dirty sticks would fall out.

 The sign liked to keep the street clean, so it would reach down and pick up the dirty sticks. The sign would put the sticks behind its secret door. It knew people would want clean sticks to burn in their fireplaces. The sign would keep the dirty sticks behind the door until it rained. Then it would hold the sticks out in the rain to clean them. It would stack the clean sticks near the road where people could pick them up to use in their fireplaces.

 The sign would then wait for more dirty sticks to put behind the secret door.

Picture:
Picture a sign (9) putting dirty sticks (36) behind it's secret door. (4)

Materials:
❑ Large Flash Cards
❑ Coloring Page 5 x 5 (Page 197)
❑ Student Book (Pages 62 and 63)
❑ Lesson Plan 32, Page 76

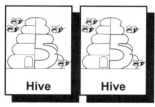

Hive x Hive =
Denty Dive

FACT 5 x 5 = 25
Hive x Hive = Denty Dive

Story:
 One very hot day, two bee hives went to a swimming pool to cool off. They had a great time. They splashed in the water and chased each other around. They even dove off the diving board, but there was a problem. They were so heavy, they made dents in the diving board when they bounced on it. The hives named their dive, denty dive, because of the denty diving board.

Picture:
Picture two hives (5 & 5) making dents in the diving board. They were doing denty dives. (25)

Materials:
❑ Large Flash Cards
❑ Coloring Page 5 x 6 (Page 199)
❑ Student Book (Pages 64 and 65)
❑ Lesson Plan 33, Page 78

FACT 5 x 6 = 30
Hive x Chicks = Dirty

Hive   Chick

Hive x Chick =
Dirty

Story:

One day some chicks were lonely. They asked a hive if it wanted to go to a nearby farm and play. The hive said, "Sure, sounds like fun!" So off they went to the farm.

They had a great time. The hive's favorite place was the pig pen. The hive and the chicks loved playing in the mud. They even rode the dirty pig and threw mud all over each other. Oh, what a great day they had playing in the mud and getting dirty!

Picture:
Picture a hive (5) and some chicks (6) getting dirty. (30)

Materials:
❑ Large Flash Cards
❑ Coloring Pages 5 x 7 (Page 199)
❑ Student Book (Page 66 and 67)
❑ Lesson Plan 34, Page 80

FACT 5 x 7 = 35
Hive x Surfin' = Dirty Dive

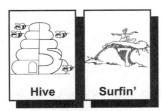

Hive   Surfin'

Hive x Surfin' =
Dirty Dive

Story:

A hive went to the beach. He was afraid of getting hurt on the rocks and the sandy beaches were too hot for his feet, so he went to a muddy beach.

The hive had a funny way of surfing at the muddy beach. He would surf up to the beach and dive right into the mud. Soon he was very dirty! The hive loved doing the dirty dives.

Picture:
Picture a hive (5) surfing (7) on a muddy beach diving into the mud. He was doing a dirty dive. (35)

Materials:
❑ Large Flash Cards
❑ Coloring Page 5 x 8 (Page 201)
❑ Student Book (Pages 68 and 69)
❑ Lesson Plan 36, Page 84

FACT 5 x 8 = 40
Hive x Skate = Fort E

Hive   **Skate**

**Hive x Skate =
Fort E**

Story:

Fort E was a fort built to look like forts of long ago. The people who lived in Fort E dressed and acted like pioneers. Visitors would come from all around to visit Fort E.

One summer day, a hive decided to skate over to Fort E. He put on his skates and went racing down the street. The people in Fort E saw the hive zooming toward them on skates and were afraid. They worried the bees from the hive would scare the visitors away, so they quickly shut the big gates to the fort. The hive tried to stop, but he couldn't. He smashed right into the side of Fort E.

Picture:

Picture a hive (5) on skates (8) smashing into the side of Fort E. (40)

Materials:
❑ Large Flash Cards
❑ Coloring Page 5 x 9 (Page 201)
❑ Student Book (Pages 70 and 71)
❑ Lesson Plan 37, Page 86

FACT 5 x 9 = 45
Hive x Sign = Fort E Dive

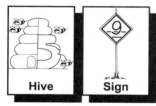

Hive   **Sign**

**Hive x Sign =
Fort E Dive**

Story:

The hive really wanted to get into Fort E. He thought and thought about it and came up with a great idea. He went to a nearby sign. He jumped into the air and onto the face of the sign. The sign bent back and then sprang forward, throwing the hive up into the air and over the high wall of Fort E. He ended up diving into Fort E.

The people in Fort E soon found out the bees in the hive were friendly. The people were very impressed with the hive's dive into the fort.

Picture:

Picture a hive (5) using a sign (9) to dive into Fort E. He did a Fort E dive. (45)

Materials:
❑ Large Flash Cards
❑ Coloring Chart 6 x 6 (Page 203)
❑ Student Book (Pages 72 and 73)
❑ Lesson Plan 38, Page 88

FACT 6 x 6 = 36
Chicks x Chicks = Dirty Chicks

Chick   Chick

**Chicks x Chicks =
Dirty Chicks**

Story:

It was a warm, sunny day. Some chicks were playing on the farm. They were scratching at the dry dirt trying to act like big chickens. It was very dusty. The chicks got very dirty. The other animals on the farm saw the chicks and said, "Chicks, chicks, dirty chicks!"

Picture:

Think chicks, (6) chicks, (6) dirty chicks! (36)

Materials:
❑ Large Flash Cards
❑ Coloring Page 6 x 7 (Page 203)
❑ Student Book (Pages 74 and 75)
❑ Lesson Plan 39, Page 90

FACT 6 x 7 = 42
Chicks x Surfin' = Fort E Zoo

Chick   Surfin'

**Chicks x Surfin' =
Fort E Zoo**

Story:

The chicks were very excited because they were going to take a school field trip to the zoo. This was no ordinary zoo. It was the zoo at Fort E. The Fort E Zoo was far away, near the ocean, so the chicks took a bus.

The bus ride was long, but soon the chicks could see the ocean and they knew they were getting close. The bus driver stopped at the beach and let the chicks get out to stretch their legs. While walking on the beach, the chicks saw a surfboard. They all thought of the same idea together, "Let's surf the rest of the way to the Fort E Zoo!" They hopped on the surfboard and surfed over to the fort. The chicks had a great day at the Fort E Zoo.

Picture:

Picture chicks (6) surfing (7) to the Fort E Zoo. (42)

Materials:
❏ Large Flash Cards
❏ Coloring Page 6 x 8 (Page 205)
❏ Cupcakes & frosting
❏ Student Book (Pages 76 and 77)
❏ Lesson Plan 40, Page 92

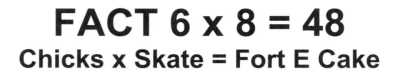

FACT 6 x 8 = 48
Chicks x Skate = Fort E Cake

Chick   Skate

Chicks x Skate =
Fort E Cake

Story:

The chicks enjoyed their visit to Fort E. When they got home, the chicks baked a cake and decorated it to look like Fort E. It even had a flag with an E on it.

One of the chicks thought of a fun way to eat the Fort E Cake. The other chicks jumped up and down when they heard the idea. The chick told them to put on their skates, race by the cake, and take a bite with their beaks.

What happened next was funny. Some of the chicks were not very good skaters, so they skated right into the side of the cake. Splat!

Picture:
Picture chicks (6) on skates (8) tasting the Fort E cake. (48)

Materials:
❏ Large Flash Cards
❏ Coloring Page 6 x 9 (Page 205)
❏ Fishing pole
❏ Gummy worms & apple
❏ Student Book (Pages 78 and 79)
❏ Lesson Plan 41, Page 94

FACT 6 x 9 = 54
Chicks x Sign = Fishing with Core

Chick   Sign

Chicks x Sign =
Fishing with Core

Story:

Some chicks had a great idea for catching tasty worms. They dreamed up a plan to go fishing for worms. The chicks knew worms liked apples. So, they found a fishing pole and attached an old apple core to the end of the fishing line. Then, they climbed to the top of a sign so they could not be seen by the worms and lowered the apple core to the ground. Yum, the chicks caught some big, juicy worms!

Picture:
Picture chicks (6) on a sign (9) fishing with a core. (54)

Materials:
❑ Large Flash Cards
❑ Coloring Chart 7 x 7 (Page 207)
❑ Student Book (Pages 80 and 81)
❑ Lesson Plan 42, Page 96

FACT 7 x 7 = 49
Surfin' x Surfin' = Fort E Twine

Surfin'   Surfin'

Surfin' x Surfin' =
Fort E Twine

Story:
The people who lived in Fort E decided to make the world's largest ball of twine. They collected twine for many years and wound it into a ball. The ball of twine became bigger and bigger. After a few years, it was almost as big as the fort. It was the biggest ball of twine in the world.

The people of the fort had a problem. The ball was so big, they could not move around. The ball was too big to roll out the gate. The people did not want to unroll the twine, because then it wouldn't be the biggest ball of twine in the world. They finally decided to move out of Fort E and leave the twine there.

The ball of twine saved their lives. Soon after they moved out, two giant waves came crashing down on Fort E and destroyed the fort and the twine.

Picture:
Picture two surfs (7) crashing down on the Fort E twine. (49)

Materials:
❑ Large Flash Cards
❑ Coloring Page 7 x 8 (Page 207)
❑ Student Book (Pages 82 and 83)
❑ Lesson Plan 43, Page 98

FACT 7 x 8 = 56
Surfin' x Skate = Fishing for Sticks

Surfin'   Skate

Surfin' x Skate =
Fishing for Sticks

Story:
There was a roller skate who always wanted to learn how to surf. One day, it went to the beach and rented a surfboard. After some instruction, the skate learned how to surf.

It surfed all day and was having so much fun it did not want to stop. Near the end of the day, the skate started getting cold. It wanted to get warm but did not want to stop surfing. It came up with an idea. The roller skate borrowed a fishing pole from a man on the beach. As it surfed along, the skate would snag sticks with the hook. When it got to the beach, it took the sticks off the hook, put them in a pile, and went surfing again. Soon the skate had enough wood to build a fire and keep warm.

Picture:
Picture skate (8) fishing for sticks (56) while he is surfing. (7)

Materials:
- ❏ Large Flash Cards
- ❏ Coloring Page 7 x 9 (Page 209)
- ❏ Student Book (Pages 84 and 85)
- ❏ Lesson Plan 44, Page 100

FACT 7 x 9 = 63
Surfin' x Sign = Sticky Bee

Surfin'   Sign

Surfin' x Sign =
Sticky Bee

Story:

      The sign saw all of its friends had learned to surf. It decided to learn to surf also. After a few lessons, the sign really liked surfing.

      Something interesting happened to the sign one day. A bee, covered with sticky honey, was just buzzing along enjoying the warm summer day when... thud! The bee flew into the sign. Neither were hurt, but the sticky bee was stuck to the sign. The sign pulled and pulled at the bee and finally pulled the bee off.

      The bee thanked the sign for helping him and flew away.

Picture:

Picture a surfing (7) sign (9) running into a sticky bee. (63)

Materials:
- ❏ Large Flash Cards
- ❏ Coloring Chart 8 x 8 (Page 209)
- ❏ Student Book (Pages 86 and 87)
- ❏ Lesson Plan 45, Page 102

FACT 8 x 8 = 64
Skate x Skate = Sticky Floor

Skate   Skate

Skate x Skate =
Sticky Floor

Story:

      Two skaters went to a skating rink. They put on their skates and started skating. After only a few seconds, they stopped moving. They didn't know what was wrong. They looked down at the floor and were shocked. The floor was covered with sticky, gooey gum. Their skates were stuck to the sticky floor.

Picture:

Picture two people on skates (8 & 8) trying to skate on a sticky floor. (64)

Materials:
❑ Large Flash Cards
❑ Coloring Page 8 x 9 (Page 211)
❑ Student Book (Pages 88 and 89)
❑ Lesson Plan 46, Page 104

FACT 8 x 9 = 72
Skate x Sign = 72 MPH

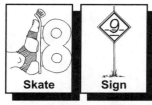

Skate   Sign

Skate x Sign = 72 MPH

Story:
    Once there was a sign who was a really fast skater. This sign was special. The speed it was skating would show up on its face. If the sign skated 10 miles per hour, a 10 showed on its face.
    One day the sign decided to skate as fast as it could. It found a deserted sidewalk and started skating. The sign skated faster and faster until it was skating 72 miles per hour.

Picture:
Picture a sign (9) on skates (8) going 72 miles per hour. (72)

Materials:
❑ Large Flash Cards
❑ Coloring Chart 9 x 9 (Page 211)
❑ Straws and construction paper
❑ Student Book (Pages 90 and 91)
❑ Lesson Plan 47, Page 106

FACT 9 x 9 = 81
Sign x Sign = Ate a Ton

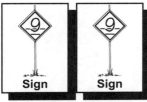

Sign   Sign

Sign x Sign = Ate a Ton

Story:
    There once was a very large man. He was a giant man. The more he ate, the bigger he grew. After many years, he was so big his silverware would not fit into his hands. He started using road signs instead of spoons. He would sit down to a meal with a sign in each hand and shovel the food in. He could eat a ton of food at a meal.

Picture:
Picture a man using to signs (9 & 9) to eat. He ate a ton (81) of food.

Education is not received. It is achieved.
Anonymous

Chapter 4
Teaching Activities

Teacher Rating
♟♟♟♟♟ Excellent
♟♟♟♟ Great
♟♟♟ Good
♟♟ Okay

1. Act Out Story - ♟♟♟♟♟
Have the students act out a multiplication fact story. Have them pretend they are the characters in the story.

2. Balloon Drawings - ♟♟
Have students draw the characters from a multiplication fact story on a deflated balloon with fine point permanent markers. Inflate the balloons and use them as characters while acting out the story.

3. Banner - ♟♟♟
Have the students design a banner for each multiplication fact. Each banner should include the fact and the picture. Display them around the room.

4. Board Game - ♟♟♟♟
Have the students design a board game using the answers to the multiplication facts to move from start to finish on the board.

5. Book - ♟♟♟♟♟
Have the students compile their artwork or fact charts into a multiplication fact book or coloring book.

6. Building Blocks - ♟♟♟
Have the students use plastic building blocks to make a model of a multiplication fact story.

7. Bulletin Board - ♟♟♟♟♟
Divide a large bulletin board into many smaller bulletin boards. As you add new multiplication facts, display the students' drawings in each section of the bulletin board.

8. Card Game - ♛♛♛♛♛
Have the students develop a card game using <u>Memorize in Minutes: The Times Tables</u> flash cards. You may use a format based on *Old Maid*, *Go Fish*, *Hearts*, *Concentration*, or some other game.

9. Cartoon - ♛♛
Have the students draw a cartoon to convey a multiplication fact story.

10. Carving - ♛♛
Have the students carve from soap a model of the characters of a multiplication fact story. Use a table knife and soft soap.

11. Charcoal Drawing - ♛♛
Have the students use charcoal to illustrate a multiplication fact story.

12. Chalk Drawings - ♛♛♛♛♛
Have the students use chalk to illustrate a multiplication fact story.

13. Cheers - ♛♛
Have the students come up with a cheer for one of the multiplication facts.

14. Chicken-wire Sculpture - ♛♛♛
As a class, build a giant model of one or more of the characters in a multiplication fact story.

15. Clay Sculptures - ♛♛♛♛♛
Have the students sculpt clay models of the objects and characters used to remember a multiplication fact story.

16. Collage - ♛♛♛
Use the students' drawings of the multiplication fact pictures to make a giant collage.

17. Coloring - ♛♛♛♛♛
Have the students color the multiplication coloring pages and organize them into a coloring book.

18. Crayon Drawings - ♛♛♛♛♛
Have the students use crayons to illustrate a multiplication fact story.

19. Colored Pencil Drawings - ♛♛♛♛♛
Have the students use colored pencils to illustrate a multiplication fact story.

20. Concentration - ♟♟♟♟

Use the flash cards to play *Concentration*. Match the answer with the picture, the answer with the fact, or the picture with the fact.

21. Costumes - ♟♟

Have the students bring in costumes or make paper costumes to add realism when they act out the stories.

22. Cross Number Puzzle - ♟♟♟♟♟

Have the students use graph paper to design a cross number puzzle using the multiplication facts. A cross number puzzle is a crossword puzzle with numbers instead of words.

23. Dance - ♟♟

Have the students create a dance that helps develop the story for one of the multiplication facts.

24. Diorama - ♟♟

Have the students build a diorama in a shoe box showing the characters in one of the multiplication stories.

25. Dirt Drawings - ♟♟♟♟♟

Find some dry dirt or sand. Let students draw a multiplication fact story in the dirt with a stick.

26. Felt Pen Drawings - ♟♟♟♟♟

Have the students use felt pens to illustrate a multiplication fact story.

27. Finger Painting - ♟♟♟♟♟

Have the students use finger paints to illustrate a multiplication fact story.

28. Flannel Board - ♟♟♟♟♟

Have the students make the scenery and characters involved in the multiplication fact stories.

29. Glitter Art - ♟♟♟♟♟

Have the students draw a multiplication fact story picture with glue, and then sprinkle colored glitter on it.

30. Greeting Card - ♟♟

Have the students design a multiplication fact greeting card.

31. Hangman - ♟♟♟♟♟

Have the students play multiplication hangman. Instead of letters, use numbers. __ x __ = __ __

32. Jig Saw Puzzle - ♛♛♛♛♛

Have the students color a fact picture. Laminate it or glue it to heavier paper. Have students cut the picture up into a jig saw puzzle for others to put together. If you use different colored paper, it is easier to tell different puzzles apart.

33. Letter Writing - ♛♛

Have the students write a letter to one of the characters in a multiplication fact story.

34. Masks - ♛♛

Have the students design a mask for the different characters in the multiplication fact stories.

35. Mobile - ♛♛

Have the students design a mobile using the pictures from the multiplication fact stories.

36. Model - ♛♛

Have the students use papier mache to build a model of the characters or events in the stories.

37. Mosaic - ♛♛♛

Have the students use small pieces of paper to illustrate one of the pictures.

38. Mural - ♛♛♛♛♛

Have the students create a giant mural of the multiplication fact stories.

39. Number Search - ♛♛♛♛

Have the students use graph paper to create a number search. A number search is like a word search with numbers instead of letters.

40. Origami - ♛♛

Have the students fold paper to create the characters in the multiplication fact stories.

41. Pantomime - ♛♛♛♛♛

Have the students pantomime a multiplication fact story while others in the class try to figure out which story it is.

42. Paper Chains - ♛♛♛♛

Have the students make a chain link for each fact. Use large links. String the multiplication chain across the room. Individual students, or groups of students, can make their own chains.

43. Pen and Ink Pen Drawings - ♛♛♛

Have the students use pen and ink to illustrate a multiplication fact story.

44. Pen Pal - ♟♟♟

Have students share <u>Memorize in Minutes: The Times Tables</u> with pen pals. Students may draw the pictures and write the stories for their pen pals.

45. Pencil Drawing - ♟♟♟

Have the students use pencil to illustrate a multiplication fact story.

46. Photograph - ♟♟

Take photographs of students acting out each multiplication fact story.

47. Pipe Cleaner People - ♟♟♟♟♟

Have the students use pipe cleaners as stick people to illustrate a multiplication fact story.

48. Play Acting - ♟♟♟♟♟

Have the students act out the multiplication fact stories for another class or parents.

49. Poem - ♟♟♟

Have the students write poems for the multiplication fact stories. Since the numbers and the pictures rhyme, poems are very easy for even young children.

50. Posters - ♟♟♟♟♟

Have the students design and illustrate a poster for each multiplication fact story.

51. Poster Paints - ♟♟♟♟♟

Have the students use poster paints to illustrate a multiplication fact story.

52. Press Conference - ♟♟

Hold an imaginary press conference with a character from a multiplication fact story.

53. Puppets - ♟♟♟

Have the students make puppets to represent the characters in the multiplication fact stories.

54. Puppet Plays - ♟♟♟♟♟

Have the students present a puppet show acting out the multiplication fact stories.

55. Rap - ♟♟

Have the students come up with a rap song for a multiplication fact story.

56. Sand Painting - ♟♟♟♟♟

Have the students make a sand painting to illustrate a multiplication fact story. Have them draw the picture with glue, and then sprinkle colored sand over it.

57. Shaving Cream Art - ♟♟♟♟♟
Spray a pile of shaving cream on each students' desk. Have students illustrate the multiplication fact stories. Shaving cream is a great desk cleaning soap.

58. Sidewalk Art - ♟♟♟♟♟
Have the students use chalk to illustrate a multiplication fact story on the sidewalk.

59. Spinner Game - ♟♟♟
Have the students design a game that uses a spinner, to quiz others on the multiplication facts.

60. Story 1 - ♟♟♟♟♟
Have the students continue the story for a multiplication fact. What happened next?

61. Story 2 - ♟♟
Have the students write a new story about a character or characters used in the multiplication fact stories.

62. Tape Recorder - ♟♟
Have the students make a recording of a multiplication fact story.

63. Test - ♟♟
Have the students design a test for the other students in the classroom.

64. Transparency - ♟♟♟♟♟
Have the students make a transparency that illustrates a multiplication fact story. Older students can develop transparencies with overlays.

65. Video - ♟♟♟♟♟
Video tape students performing a multiplication fact story. Better yet, have students video tape other students.

66. Water Color Painting - ♟♟♟♟♟
Have the students use water colors to illustrate a multiplication fact story.

67. Yarn Art - ♟♟♟♟♟
Have the students design a picture of a multiplication fact using yarn glued to a piece of paper.

Chapter 5
Tests and Quizzes

Tests and quizzes let you know what facts need to be reviewed. The goal is for every student to get every problem right. You want student success! When you give a test or quiz, make sure that students are not tempted to look at their neighbors papers. Have them move their desks apart or move to where they are not tempted to share answers.

When correcting a quiz, you may want to have the students exchange papers and correct each other's papers, however the tests should be corrected by an adult.

The quizzes and tests should be given weekly for months after all the students have achieved 100% accuracy.
Remember, YOU CANNOT OVER TEACH the multiplication facts.

Pre-Test 0-9

Name_____

Date _____ Score_____

1) 2×5	2) 6×2	3) 3×6	4) 7×3	5) 4×8	6) 9×4	7) 6×7	8) 8×6	9) 9×9
10) 4×2	11) 2×7	12) 5×3	13) 3×8	14) 7×4	15) 5×5	16) 6×6	17) 6×9	18) 9×8
19) 2×3	20) 8×2	21) 3×4	22) 9×3	23) 4×6	24) 6×5	25) 5×9	26) 7×7	27) 8×8
28) 2×2	29) 2×9	30) 3×3	31) 4×4	32) 5×4	33) 5×7	34) 8×5	35) 7×8	36) 9×7
37) 7×7	38) 9×6	39) 4×7	40) 6×4	41) 2×8	42) 7×2	43) 4×1	44) 1×3	45) 1×0
46) 8×7	47) 6×8	48) 8×4	49) 4×5	50) 9×2	51) 2×6	52) 1×5	53) 2×1	54) 0×2
55) 7×9	56) 7×6	57) 4×9	58) 4×4	59) 3×3	60) 5×2	61) 6×1	62) 1×1	63) 3×0
64) 8×8	65) 6×6	66) 5×5	67) 3×9	68) 4×3	69) 2×4	70) 1×7	71) 9×0	72) 0×4
73) 8×9	74) 9×5	75) 5×6	76) 8×3	77) 3×5	78) 3×2	79) 8×1	80) 0×8	81) 5×0
82) 9×9	83) 5×8	84) 7×5	85) 3×7	86) 6×3	87) 2×2	88) 1×9	89) 7×0	90) 0×6

Picture Quiz 1

Name_____

Date _____ Score_____

Draw the picture for the number **2**.	Draw the picture for the number **3**.	Draw the picture for the number **4**.
Draw the picture for the number **5**.	Draw the picture for the number **6**.	Draw the picture for the number **7**.
Draw the picture for the number **8**.	Draw the picture for the number **9**.	

Picture Quiz 2

Name_____

Date _____ Score_____

In this box, draw the picture for **2 x 2**.	In this box, draw the picture for **2 x 3** (and 3 x 2).	In this box, draw the picture for **2 x 4** (and 4 x 2).
In this box, draw the picture for **2 x 5** (and 5 x 2).	In this box, draw the picture for **2 x 6** (and 6 x 2).	In this box, draw the picture for **2 x 7** (and 7 x 2).
In this box, draw the picture for **2 x 8** (and 8 x 2).	In this box, draw the picture for **2 x 9** (and 9 x 2).	In this box, draw the picture for **3 x 3**.
In this box, draw the picture for **3 x 4** (and 4 x 3).	In this box, draw the picture for **3 x 5** (and 5 x 3).	In this box, draw the picture for **3 x 6** (and 6 x 3).

	Picture Quiz 3		Name_____
			Date _____ Score_____

In this box, draw the picture for **3 x 7** (and 7 x 3).	In this box, draw the picture for **3 x 8** (and 8 x 3).	In this box, draw the picture for **3 x 9** (and 9 x 3).
In this box, draw the picture for **4 x 4.**	In this box, draw the picture for **4 x 5** (and 5 x 4).	In this box, draw the picture for **4 x 6** (and 6 x 4).
In this box, draw the picture for **4 x 7** (and 7 x 4).	In this box, draw the picture for **4 x 8** (and 8 x 4).	In this box, draw the picture for **4 x 9** (and 9 x 4).
In this box, draw the picture for **5 x 5.**	In this box, draw the picture for **5 x 6** (and 6 x 5).	In this box, draw the picture for **5 x 7** (and 7 x 5).

| Picture Quiz 4 | Name_____ |
| | Date _____ Score_____ |

In this box, draw the picture for **5 x 8** (and 8 x 5).	In this box, draw the picture for **5 x 9** (and 9 x 5).	In this box, draw the picture for **6 x 6**.
In this box, draw the picture for **6 x 7** (and 7 x 6).	In this box, draw the picture for **6 x 8** (and 8 x 6).	In this box, draw the picture for **6 x 9** (and 9 x 6).
In this box, draw the picture for **7 x 7**.	In this box, draw the picture for **7 x 8** (and 8 x 7).	In this box, draw the picture for **7 x 9** (and 9 x 7).
In this box, draw the picture for **8 x 8**.	In this box, draw the picture for **8 x 9** (and 9 x 8).	In this box, draw the picture for **9 x 9**.

Quick Quiz 1

Name_____
Date _____ Score_____
Facts _____ *0 through 1* _____

1) 4 x 0	2) 0 x 5	3) 1 x 3	4) 6 x 1	5) 2 x 0	6) 0 x 7	7) 1 x 1	8) 8 x 1	9) 0 x 9
10) 1 x 5	11) 2 x 1	12) 7 x 0	13) 1 x 0	14) 1 x 9	15) 8 x 0	16) 1 x 4	17) 0 x 2	18) 0 x 3
19) 1 x 6	20) 0 x 4	21) 1 x 8	22) 3 x 0	23) 0 x 1	24) 0 x 6	25) 5 x 1	26) 7 x 1	27) 0 x 8
28) 5 x 0	29) 9 x 1	30) 3 x 1	31) 4 x 1	32) 0 x 0	33) 1 x 7	34) 6 x 0	35) 9 x 0	36) 1 x 2

Quick Quiz 2

Name_____
Date _____ Score_____
Facts _____ *0 through 2* _____

1) 1 x 2	2) 9 x 1	3) 2 x 2	4) 0 x 1	5) 3 x 2	6) 1 x 8	7) 2 x 4	8) 2 x 0	9) 5 x 2
10) 7 x 1	11) 2 x 6	12) 0 x 3	13) 7 x 2	14) 1 x 6	15) 2 x 8	16) 4 x 0	17) 9 x 2	18) 5 x 1
19) 2 x 9	20) 0 x 5	21) 8 x 2	22) 1 x 4	23) 2 x 7	24) 6 x 0	25) 6 x 2	26) 3 x 1	27) 2 x 5
28) 0 x 7	29) 4 x 2	30) 8 x 1	31) 2 x 3	32) 8 x 0	33) 2 x 2	34) 1 x 1	35) 0 x 0	36) 0 x 9

Quick Quiz 3

Name_____
Date _____ Score_____
Facts _____ *0 through 3*

1) 3 x2	2) 9 x2	3) 3 x3	4) 1 x9	5) 3 x4	6) 0 x2	7) 5 x3	8) 8 x1	9) 3 x6
10) 2 x8	11) 7 x3	12) 1 x7	13) 3 x8	14) 7 x2	15) 9 x3	16) 6 x1	17) 3 x1	18) 8 x0
19) 3 x9	20) 1 x5	21) 8 x3	22) 2 x6	23) 3 x7	24) 4 x1	25) 6 x3	26) 0 x4	27) 3 x5
28) 5 x2	29) 2 x3	30) 2 x4	31) 3 x3	32) 2 x1	33) 4 x3	34) 9 x0	35) 2 x2	36) 8 x2

Quick Quiz 4

Name_____
Date _____ Score_____
Facts _____ *0 through 4*

1) 1 x4	2) 9 x3	3) 4 x2	4) 2 x2	5) 3 x4	6) 3 x8	7) 4 x4	8) 2 x3	9) 5 x4
10) 7 x3	11) 4 x6	12) 2 x4	13) 7 x4	14) 3 x6	15) 4 x8	16) 9 x1	17) 9 x4	18) 5 x3
19) 4 x9	20) 0 x5	21) 8 x4	22) 4 x3	23) 4 x7	24) 5 x2	25) 6 x4	26) 3 x3	27) 4 x5
28) 2 x6	29) 4 x4	30) 3 x2	31) 1 x7	32) 8 x2	33) 6 x1	34) 9 x2	35) 4 x0	36) 7 x2

Quick Quiz 5

Name_____
Date _____ Score_____
Facts _____0 through 5_____

1) 5×5	2) 2×9	3) 5×6	4) 8×3	5) 7×5	6) 4×7	7) 5×8	8) 6×1	9) 9×5
10) 3×4	11) 5×4	12) 2×3	13) 3×5	14) 4×9	15) 5×2	16) 8×2	17) 1×5	18) 3×7
19) 5×9	20) 6×4	21) 8×5	22) 2×7	23) 5×7	24) 2×2	25) 6×5	26) 6×2	27) 4×5
28) 6×3	29) 5×0	30) 9×3	31) 2×5	32) 4×4	33) 8×4	34) 4×2	35) 0×7	36) 3×3

Quick Quiz 6

Name_____
Date _____ Score_____
Facts _____2 through 6_____

1) 6×5	2) 2×2	3) 9×6	4) 3×9	5) 6×8	6) 4×4	7) 7×6	8) 5×9	9) 6×6
10) 3×2	11) 4×6	12) 8×3	13) 6×3	14) 5×4	15) 2×6	16) 8×5	17) 6×7	18) 2×4
19) 8×6	20) 3×7	21) 6×9	22) 7×4	23) 6×1	24) 5×7	25) 6×4	26) 3×3	27) 5×6
28) 4×8	29) 5×2	30) 9×4	31) 5×5	32) 4×3	33) 9×2	34) 3×5	35) 7×2	36) 2×8

Quick Quiz 7

Name_____
Date _____ Score_____
Facts _____ *2 through 7* _____

1) 9 x 7	2) 2 x 2	3) 7 x 8	4) 3 x 9	5) 4 x 4	6) 5 x 9	7) 2 x 8	8) 6 x 3	9) 5 x 5
10) 7 x 6	11) 3 x 3	12) 6 x 8	13) 4 x 8	14) 5 x 2	15) 8 x 3	16) 4 x 6	17) 8 x 7	18) 9 x 2
19) 7 x 7	20) 3 x 2	21) 5 x 4	22) 8 x 5	23) 9 x 6	24) 2 x 4	25) 7 x 4	26) 7 x 7	27) 3 x 5
28) 7 x 2	29) 4 x 3	30) 3 x 7	31) 7 x 9	32) 2 x 6	33) 5 x 7	34) 9 x 4	35) 6 x 5	36) 6 x 6

Quick Quiz 8

Name_____
Date _____ Score_____
Facts _____ *2 through 8* _____

1) 8 x 8	2) 9 x 5	3) 9 x 8	4) 2 x 2	5) 6 x 4	6) 2 x 5	7) 5 x 8	8) 6 x 6	9) 3 x 4
10) 7 x 8	11) 7 x 3	12) 2 x 9	13) 8 x 6	14) 4 x 4	15) 3 x 8	16) 7 x 7	17) 2 x 3	18) 4 x 9
19) 8 x 4	20) 5 x 5	21) 9 x 7	22) 3 x 6	23) 7 x 5	24) 8 x 2	25) 5 x 6	26) 3 x 3	27) 6 x 7
28) 4 x 5	29) 6 x 9	30) 2 x 7	31) 5 x 3	32) 4 x 2	33) 8 x 9	34) 4 x 7	35) 9 x 3	36) 6 x 2

Quick Quiz 9a

Name_____
Date _____ Score_____
Facts _____ *2 through 9* _____

1) 9 x 2	2) 5 x 5	3) 8 x 7	4) 6 x 3	5) 9 x 9	6) 5 x 7	7) 2 x 4	8) 9 x 4	9) 6 x 6
10) 3 x 2	11) 9 x 6	12) 8 x 3	13) 7 x 7	14) 5 x 2	15) 6 x 8	16) 5 x 9	17) 4 x 4	18) 9 x 8
19) 3 x 3	20) 4 x 8	21) 2 x 6	22) 8 x 8	23) 3 x 7	24) 7 x 4	25) 2 x 2	26) 8 x 5	27) 7 x 9
28) 5 x 4	29) 2 x 8	30) 6 x 5	31) 4 x 3	32) 7 x 2	33) 3 x 5	34) 7 x 6	35) 3 x 9	36) 4 x 6

Quick Quiz 9b

Name_____
Date _____ Score_____
Facts _____ *2 through 9* _____

1) 9 x 5	2) 4 x 4	3) 2 x 7	4) 7 x 8	5) 2 x 3	6) 9 x 9	7) 5 x 3	8) 4 x 9	9) 6 x 6
10) 7 x 3	11) 8 x 9	12) 3 x 3	13) 6 x 4	14) 2 x 9	15) 5 x 8	16) 7 x 5	17) 2 x 5	18) 8 x 8
19) 3 x 8	20) 5 x 5	21) 6 x 9	22) 4 x 2	23) 8 x 6	24) 9 x 3	25) 2 x 2	26) 4 x 7	27) 9 x 7
28) 6 x 2	29) 4 x 5	30) 7 x 7	31) 8 x 2	32) 6 x 7	33) 3 x 4	34) 5 x 6	35) 8 x 4	36) 3 x 6

Post-Test 0-9

Name_____

Date _____ Score_____

1) 9 x 9	2) 6 x 8	3) 7 x 6	4) 4 x 9	5) 8 x 4	6) 3 x 7	7) 6 x 3	8) 2 x 6	9) 5 x 2
10) 8 x 9	11) 9 x 6	12) 6 x 6	13) 5 x 5	14) 4 x 7	15) 8 x 3	16) 3 x 5	17) 7 x 2	18) 2 x 4
19) 8 x 8	20) 7 x 7	21) 9 x 5	22) 5 x 6	23) 6 x 4	24) 3 x 9	25) 4 x 3	26) 2 x 8	27) 3 x 2
28) 9 x 7	29) 8 x 7	30) 5 x 8	31) 7 x 5	32) 4 x 5	33) 4 x 4	34) 3 x 3	35) 9 x 2	36) 2 x 2
37) 7 x 7	38) 6 x 9	39) 7 x 4	40) 4 x 6	41) 8 x 2	42) 2 x 7	43) 1 x 4	44) 3 x 1	45) 0 x 1
46) 7 x 8	47) 8 x 6	48) 4 x 8	49) 5 x 4	50) 2 x 9	51) 6 x 2	52) 5 x 1	53) 1 x 2	54) 2 x 0
55) 9 x 7	56) 6 x 7	57) 9 x 4	58) 4 x 4	59) 3 x 3	60) 2 x 5	61) 1 x 6	62) 1 x 1	63) 0 x 3
64) 8 x 8	65) 6 x 6	66) 5 x 5	67) 9 x 3	68) 3 x 4	69) 4 x 2	70) 7 x 1	71) 0 x 9	72) 4 x 0
73) 9 x 8	74) 5 x 9	75) 6 x 5	76) 3 x 8	77) 5 x 3	78) 2 x 3	79) 1 x 8	80) 8 x 0	81) 0 x 5
82) 9 x 9	83) 8 x 5	84) 5 x 7	85) 7 x 3	86) 3 x 6	87) 2 x 2	88) 9 x 1	89) 0 x 7	90) 6 x 0

Using Review Quizzes

The review quizzes are designed to be used for added review after your students have learned the multiplication facts.

The multiplication facts are in order from 2 x 2 to 9 x 9 on each quiz. Figure 5-1 and 5-2 below show the order of the facts.

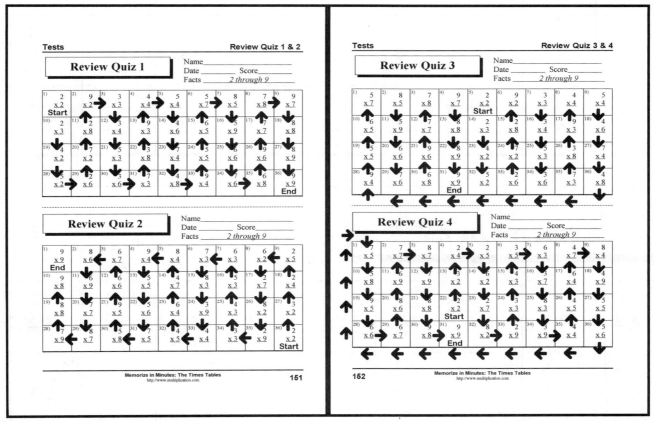

Figure 5-1   Figure 5-2

Review Quiz 1

Name_____
Date _____ Score_____
Facts _____ *2 through 9* _____

1) 2 x 2	2) 9 x 2	3) 3 x 3	4) 4 x 4	5) 5 x 4	6) 5 x 7	7) 8 x 5	8) 7 x 8	9) 9 x 7
10) 2 x 3	11) 2 x 8	12) 3 x 4	13) 9 x 3	14) 4 x 6	15) 6 x 5	16) 5 x 9	17) 7 x 7	18) 8 x 8
19) 4 x 2	20) 7 x 2	21) 5 x 3	22) 3 x 8	23) 7 x 4	24) 5 x 5	25) 6 x 6	26) 9 x 6	27) 8 x 9
28) 5 x 2	29) 2 x 6	30) 3 x 6	31) 7 x 3	32) 4 x 8	33) 9 x 4	34) 7 x 6	35) 6 x 8	36) 9 x 9

Review Quiz 2

Name_____
Date _____ Score_____
Facts _____ *2 through 9* _____

1) 9 x 9	2) 8 x 6	3) 6 x 7	4) 9 x 4	5) 8 x 4	6) 7 x 3	7) 6 x 3	8) 6 x 2	9) 2 x 5
10) 9 x 8	11) 6 x 9	12) 6 x 6	13) 5 x 5	14) 4 x 7	15) 8 x 3	16) 5 x 3	17) 2 x 7	18) 2 x 4
19) 8 x 8	20) 7 x 7	21) 9 x 5	22) 5 x 6	23) 6 x 4	24) 3 x 9	25) 4 x 3	26) 8 x 2	27) 3 x 2
28) 7 x 9	29) 8 x 7	30) 5 x 8	31) 7 x 5	32) 4 x 5	33) 4 x 4	34) 3 x 3	35) 2 x 9	36) 2 x 2

Review Quiz 3

Name_____
Date _____ Score_____
Facts _____ *2 through 9*

1) 5 x 7	2) 8 x 5	3) 7 x 8	4) 9 x 7	5) 2 x 2	6) 9 x 2	7) 3 x 3	8) 4 x 4	9) 5 x 4
10) 6 x 5	11) 5 x 9	12) 7 x 7	13) 8 x 8	14) 2 x 3	15) 2 x 8	16) 3 x 4	17) 9 x 3	18) 4 x 6
19) 5 x 5	20) 6 x 6	21) 9 x 6	22) 8 x 9	23) 4 x 2	24) 7 x 2	25) 5 x 3	26) 3 x 8	27) 7 x 4
28) 9 x 4	29) 7 x 6	30) 6 x 8	31) 9 x 9	32) 5 x 2	33) 2 x 6	34) 3 x 6	35) 7 x 3	36) 4 x 8

Review Quiz 4

Name_____
Date _____ Score_____
Facts _____ *2 through 9*

1) 7 x 5	2) 7 x 7	3) 8 x 7	4) 2 x 4	5) 2 x 5	6) 3 x 5	7) 6 x 3	8) 4 x 7	9) 8 x 4
10) 5 x 8	11) 6 x 9	12) 7 x 9	13) 3 x 2	14) 6 x 2	15) 4 x 3	16) 3 x 7	17) 6 x 4	18) 4 x 9
19) 9 x 5	20) 8 x 6	21) 8 x 8	22) 2 x 2	23) 2 x 7	24) 3 x 3	25) 8 x 3	26) 4 x 5	27) 5 x 5
28) 6 x 6	29) 6 x 7	30) 9 x 8	31) 9 x 9	32) 8 x 2	33) 2 x 9	34) 3 x 9	35) 4 x 4	36) 5 x 6

Pre-Test 0-9

1. 2 x 5 = **10**	2. 6 x 2 = **12**	3. 3 x 6 = **18**	4. 7 x 3 = **21**	5. 4 x 8 = **32**	6. 9 x 4 = **36**	7. 6 x 7 = **42**	8. 8 x 6 = **48**	9. 9 x 9 = **81**
10. 4 x 2 = **8**	11. 2 x 7 = **14**	12. 5 x 3 = **15**	13. 3 x 8 = **24**	14. 7 x 4 = **28**	15. 5 x 5 = **25**	16. 6 x 6 = **36**	17. 6 x 9 = **54**	18. 9 x 8 = **72**
19. 2 x 3 = **6**	20. 8 x 2 = **16**	21. 3 x 4 = **12**	22. 9 x 3 = **27**	23. 4 x 6 = **24**	24. 6 x 5 = **30**	25. 5 x 9 = **45**	26. 7 x 7 = **49**	27. 8 x 8 = **64**
28. 2 x 2 = **4**	29. 2 x 9 = **18**	30. 3 x 3 = **9**	31. 4 x 4 = **16**	32. 5 x 4 = **20**	33. 5 x 7 = **35**	34. 8 x 5 = **40**	35. 7 x 8 = **56**	36. 9 x 7 = **63**
37. 7 x 7 = **49**	38. 9 x 6 = **54**	39. 4 x 7 = **28**	40. 6 x 4 = **24**	41. 2 x 8 = **16**	42. 7 x 2 = **14**	43. 4 x 1 = **4**	44. 1 x 3 = **3**	45. 1 x 0 = **0**
46. 8 x 7 = **56**	47. 6 x 8 = **48**	48. 8 x 4 = **32**	49. 4 x 5 = **20**	50. 9 x 2 = **18**	51. 2 x 6 = **12**	52. 1 x 5 = **5**	53. 2 x 1 = **2**	54. 0 x 2 = **0**
55. 7 x 9 = **63**	56. 7 x 6 = **42**	57. 4 x 9 = **36**	58. 4 x 4 = **16**	59. 3 x 3 = **9**	60. 5 x 2 = **10**	61. 6 x 1 = **6**	62. 1 x 1 = **1**	63. 3 x 0 = **0**
64. 8 x 8 = **64**	65. 6 x 6 = **36**	66. 5 x 5 = **25**	67. 3 x 9 = **27**	68. 4 x 3 = **12**	69. 2 x 4 = **8**	70. 1 x 7 = **7**	71. 9 x 0 = **0**	72. 0 x 4 = **0**
73. 8 x 9 = **72**	74. 9 x 5 = **45**	75. 5 x 6 = **30**	76. 8 x 3 = **24**	77. 3 x 5 = **15**	78. 3 x 2 = **6**	79. 8 x 1 = **8**	80. 0 x 8 = **0**	81. 5 x 0 = **0**
82. 9 x 9 = **81**	83. 5 x 8 = **40**	84. 7 x 5 = **35**	85. 3 x 7 = **21**	86. 6 x 3 = **18**	87. 2 x 2 = **4**	88. 1 x 9 = **9**	89. 7 x 0 = **0**	90. 0 x 6 = **0**

Post-Test 0-9

1. 9 x 9 = **81**	2. 6 x 8 = **48**	3. 7 x 6 = **42**	4. 4 x 9 = **36**	5. 8 x 4 = **32**	6. 3 x 7 = **21**	7. 6 x 3 = **18**	8. 2 x 6 = **12**	9. 5 x 2 = **10**
10. 8 x 9 = **72**	11. 9 x 6 = **54**	12. 6 x 6 = **36**	13. 5 x 5 = **25**	14. 4 x 7 = **28**	15. 8 x 3 = **24**	16. 3 x 5 = **15**	17. 7 x 2 = **14**	18. 2 x 4 = **8**
19. 8 x 8 = **64**	20. 7 x 7 = **49**	21. 9 x 5 = **45**	22. 5 x 6 = **30**	23. 6 x 4 = **24**	24. 3 x 9 = **27**	25. 4 x 3 = **12**	26. 2 x 8 = **16**	27. 3 x 2 = **6**
28. 9 x 7 = **63**	29. 8 x 7 = **56**	30. 5 x 8 = **40**	31. 7 x 5 = **35**	32. 4 x 5 = **20**	33. 4 x 4 = **16**	34. 3 x 3 = **9**	35. 9 x 2 = **18**	36. 2 x 2 = **4**
37. 7 x 7 = **49**	38. 6 x 9 = **54**	39. 7 x 4 = **28**	40. 4 x 6 = **24**	41. 8 x 2 = **16**	42. 2 x 7 = **14**	43. 1 x 4 = **4**	44. 3 x 1 = **3**	45. 0 x 1 = **0**
46. 7 x 8 = **56**	47. 8 x 6 = **48**	48. 4 x 8 = **32**	49. 5 x 4 = **20**	50. 2 x 9 = **18**	51. 6 x 2 = **12**	52. 5 x 1 = **5**	53. 1 x 2 = **2**	54. 2 x 0 = **0**
55. 9 x 7 = **63**	56. 6 x 7 = **42**	57. 9 x 4 = **36**	58. 4 x 4 = **16**	59. 3 x 3 = **9**	60. 2 x 5 = **10**	61. 1 x 6 = **6**	62. 1 x 1 = **1**	63. 0 x 3 = **0**
64. 8 x 8 = **64**	65. 6 x 6 = **36**	66. 5 x 5 = **25**	67. 9 x 3 = **27**	68. 3 x 4 = **12**	69. 4 x 2 = **8**	70. 7 x 1 = **7**	71. 0 x 9 = **0**	72. 4 x 0 = **0**
73. 9 x 8 = **72**	74. 5 x 9 = **45**	75. 6 x 5 = **30**	76. 3 x 8 = **24**	77. 5 x 3 = **15**	78. 2 x 3 = **6**	79. 1 x 8 = **8**	80. 8 x 0 = **0**	81. 0 x 5 = **0**
82. 9 x 9 = **81**	83. 8 x 5 = **40**	84. 5 x 7 = **35**	85. 7 x 3 = **21**	86. 3 x 6 = **18**	87. 2 x 2 = **4**	88. 9 x 1 = **9**	89. 0 x 7 = **0**	90. 6 x 0 = **0**

Quick Quiz 1

1) **0**	2) **0**	3) **3**	4) **6**	5) **0**	6) **0**	7) **1**	8) **8**	9) **0**
10) **5**	11) **2**	12) **0**	13) **0**	14) **9**	15) **0**	16) **4**	17) **0**	18) **0**
19) **6**	20) **0**	21) **8**	22) **0**	23) **0**	24) **0**	25) **5**	26) **7**	27) **0**
28) **0**	29) **9**	30) **3**	31) **4**	32) **0**	33) **7**	34) **0**	35) **0**	36) **2**

Quick Quiz 2

1) **2**	2) **9**	3) **4**	4) **0**	5) **6**	6) **8**	7) **8**	8) **0**	9) **10**
10) **7**	11) **12**	12) **0**	13) **14**	14) **6**	15) **16**	16) **0**	17) **18**	18) **5**
19) **18**	20) **0**	21) **16**	22) **4**	23) **14**	24) **0**	25) **12**	26) **3**	27) **10**
28) **0**	29) **8**	30) **8**	31) **6**	32) **0**	33) **4**	34) **1**	35) **0**	36) **0**

Quick Quiz 3

1) **6**	2) **18**	3) **9**	4) **9**	5) **12**	6) **0**	7) **15**	8) **8**	9) **18**
10) **16**	11) **21**	12) **7**	13) **24**	14) **14**	15) **27**	16) **6**	17) **3**	18) **0**
19) **27**	20) **5**	21) **24**	22) **12**	23) **21**	24) **4**	25) **18**	26) **0**	27) **15**
28) **10**	29) **6**	30) **8**	31) **9**	32) **2**	33) **12**	34) **0**	35) **4**	36) **16**

Quick Quiz 4

1) **4**	2) **27**	3) **8**	4) **4**	5) **12**	6) **24**	7) **16**	8) **6**	9) **20**
10) **21**	11) **24**	12) **8**	13) **28**	14) **18**	15) **32**	16) **9**	17) **36**	18) **15**
19) **36**	20) **0**	21) **32**	22) **12**	23) **28**	24) **10**	25) **24**	26) **9**	27) **20**
28) **12**	29) **16**	30) **6**	31) **7**	32) **16**	33) **6**	34) **18**	35) **0**	36) **14**

Quick Quiz 5

1) **25**	2) **18**	3) **30**	4) **24**	5) **35**	6) **28**	7) **40**	8) **6**	9) **45**
10) **12**	11) **20**	12) **6**	13) **15**	14) **36**	15) **10**	16) **16**	17) **5**	18) **21**
19) **45**	20) **24**	21) **40**	22) **14**	23) **35**	24) **4**	25) **30**	26) **12**	27) **20**
28) **18**	29) **0**	30) **27**	31) **10**	32) **16**	33) **32**	34) **8**	35) **0**	36) **9**

Quick Quiz 6

1) **30**	2) **4**	3) **54**	4) **27**	5) **48**	6) **16**	7) **42**	8) **45**	9) **36**
10) **6**	11) **24**	12) **24**	13) **18**	14) **20**	15) **12**	16) **40**	17) **42**	18) **8**
19) **48**	20) **21**	21) **54**	22) **28**	23) **6**	24) **35**	25) **24**	26) **9**	27) **30**
28) **32**	29) **10**	30) **36**	31) **25**	32) **12**	33) **18**	34) **15**	35) **14**	36) **16**

Quick Quiz 7

1) **63**	2) **4**	3) **56**	4) **27**	5) **16**	6) **45**	7) **16**	8) **18**	9) **25**
10) **42**	11) **9**	12) **48**	13) **32**	14) **10**	15) **24**	16) **24**	17) **56**	18) **18**
19) **49**	20) **6**	21) **20**	22) **40**	23) **54**	24) **8**	25) **28**	26) **49**	27) **15**
28) **14**	29) **12**	30) **21**	31) **63**	32) **12**	33) **35**	34) **36**	35) **30**	36) **36**

Quick Quiz 8
1) 64   2) 45   3) 72   4) 4   5) 24   6) 10   7) 40   8) 36   9) 12
10) 56   11) 21   12) 18   13) 48   14) 16   15) 24   16) 49   17) 6   18) 36
19) 32   20) 25   21) 63   22) 18   23) 35   24) 16   25) 30   26) 9   27) 42
28) 20   29) 54   30) 14   31) 15   32) 8   33) 72   34) 28   35) 27   36) 12

Quick Quiz 9a
1) 18   2) 25   3) 56   4) 18   5) 81   6) 35   7) 8   8) 36   9) 36
10) 6   11) 54   12) 24   13) 49   14) 10   15) 48   16) 45   17) 16   18) 72
19) 9   20) 32   21) 12   22) 64   23) 21   24) 28   25) 4   26) 40   27) 63
28) 20   29) 16   30) 30   31) 12   32) 14   33) 15   34) 42   35) 27   36) 24

Quick Quiz 9b
1) 45   2) 16   3) 14   4) 56   5) 6   6) 81   7) 15   8) 36   9) 36
10) 21   11) 72   12) 9   13) 24   14) 18   15) 40   16) 35   17) 10   18) 64
19) 24   20) 25   21) 54   22) 8   23) 48   24) 27   25) 4   26) 28   27) 63
28) 12   29) 20   30) 49   31) 16   32) 42   33) 12   34) 30   35) 32   36) 18

Review Quiz 1
1) 4   2) 18   3) 9   4) 16   5) 20   6) 35   7) 40   8) 56   9) 63
10) 6   11) 16   12) 12   13) 27   14) 24   15) 30   16) 45   17) 49   18) 64
19) 8   20) 14   21) 15   22) 24   23) 28   24) 25   25) 36   26) 54   27) 72
28) 10   29) 12   30) 18   31) 21   32) 32   33) 36   34) 42   35) 48   36) 81

Review Quiz 2
1) 81   2) 48   3) 42   4) 36   5) 32   6) 21   7) 18   8) 12   9) 10
10) 72   11) 54   12) 36   13) 25   14) 28   15) 24   16) 15   17) 14   18) 8
19) 64   20) 49   21) 45   22) 30   23) 24   24) 27   25) 12   26) 16   27) 6
28) 63   29) 56   30) 40   31) 35   32) 20   33) 16   34) 9   35) 18   36) 4

Review Quiz 3
1) 35   2) 40   3) 56   4) 63   5) 4   6) 18   7) 9   8) 16   9) 20
10) 30   11) 45   12) 49   13) 64   14) 6   15) 16   16) 12   17) 27   18) 24
19) 25   20) 36   21) 54   22) 72   23) 8   24) 14   25) 15   26) 24   27) 28
28) 36   29) 42   30) 48   31) 81   32) 10   33) 12   34) 18   35) 21   36) 32

Review Quiz 4
1) 35   2) 49   3) 56   4) 8   5) 10   6) 15   7) 18   8) 28   9) 32
10) 40   11) 54   12) 63   13) 6   14) 12   15) 12   16) 21   17) 24   18) 36
19) 45   20) 48   21) 64   22) 4   23) 14   24) 9   25) 24   26) 20   27) 25
28) 36   29) 42   30) 72   31) 81   32) 16   33) 18   34) 27   35) 16   36) 30

Chapter 6
Quick View

The Quick View pages give you an overview of each series of multiplication facts.

2

2 = Shoe

2 x 2 = 4

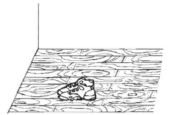

Shoe x Shoe = Floor

2 x 3 = 6

Shoe x Tree = Sticks

2 x 4 = 8

Shoe x Door = Plate

2 x 5 = 10

Shoe x Hive = Pen

2 x 6 = 12

Shoe x Chicks = Elf

2 x 7 = 14

Shoe x Surfin' = Four Kings

2 x 8 = 16

Shoe x Skate = Sick Queen

2 x 9 = 18

Shoe x Sign = Aching

3

3 = Tree

3 x 2 = 6

Tree x Shoe = Sticks

3 x 3 = 9

Tree x Tree = Line

3 x 4 = 12

Tree x Door = Elf

3 x 5 = 15

Tree x Hive = Lifting

3 x 6 = 18

Tree x Chicks = Aching

3 x 7 = 21

Tree x Surfin' = Denty Sun

3 x 8 = 24

Tree x Skate = Denty Floor

3 x 9 = 27

Tree x Sign = Denty Chef's Van

4

4 = Door

4 x 2 = 8

Door x Shoe = Plate

4 x 3 = 12

Door x Tree = Elf

4 x 4 = 16

Door x Door = Sick Queen

4 x 5 = 20

Door x Hive = Honey

4 x 6 = 24

Door x Chicks = Denty Floor

4 x 7 = 28

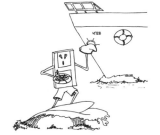

Door x Surfin' = Denty Plate

4 x 8 = 32

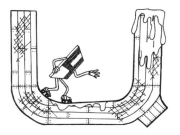

Door x Skate = Dirty U

4 x 9 = 36

Door x Sign = Dirty Sticks

5

5 = Hive

5 x 2 = 10

Hive x Shoe =
Pen

5 x 3 = 15

Hive x Tree =
Lifting

5 x 4 = 20

Hive x Door =
Honey

5 x 5 = 25

Hive x Hive =
Denty Dive

5 x 6 = 30

Hive x Chicks =
Dirty

5 x 7 = 35

Hive x Surfin' =
Dirty Dive

5 x 8 = 40

Hive x Skate =
Fort E

5 x 9 = 45

Hive x Sign =
Fort E Dive

6

6 = Chick

6 x 2 = 12

Chick x Shoe = Elf

6 x 3 = 18

Chicks x Tree = Aching

6 x 4 = 24

Chicks x Door = Denty Floor

6 x 5 = 30

Chicks x Hive = Dirty

6 x 6 = 36

Chicks x Chicks = Dirty Chicks

6 x 7 = 42

Chicks x Surfin' = Fort E Zoo

6 x 8 = 48

Chicks x Skate = Fort E Cake

6 x 9 = 54

Chicks x Sign = Fishing with Core

7

7 = Surfin'

7 x 2 = 14

**Surfin' x Shoe =
Four Kings**

7 x 3 = 21

**Surfin' x Tree =
Denty Sun**

7 x 4 = 28

**Surfin' x Door =
Denty Plate**

7 x 5 = 35

**Surfin' x Hive =
Dirty Dive**

7 x 6 = 42

**Surfin' x Chicks =
Fort E Zoo**

7 x 7 = 49

**Surfin' x Surfin' =
Fort E Twine**

7 x 8 = 56

**Surfin' x Skate =
Fishing for Sticks**

7 x 9 = 63

**Surfin' x Sign =
Sticky Bee**

8

8 = Skate

8 x 2 = 16

Skate x Shoe = Sick Queen

8 x 3 = 24

Skate x Tree = Denty Floor

8 x 4 = 32

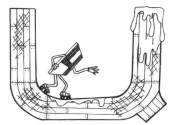

Skate x Door = Dirty U

8 x 5 = 40

Skate x Hive = Fort E

8 x 6 = 48

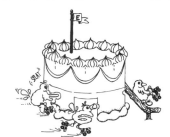

Skate x Chicks = Fort E Cake

8 x 7 = 56

Skate x Surfin' = Fishing for Sticks

8 x 8 = 64

Skate x Skate = Sticky Floor

8 x 9 = 72

Skate x Sign = 72 MPH

9

9 = Sign

9 x 2 = 18

Sign x Shoe = Aching

9 x 3 = 27

Sign x Tree = Denty Chef's Van

9 x 4 = 36

Sign x Door = Dirty Sticks

9 x 5 = 45

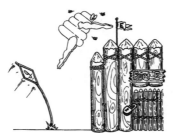

Sign x Hive = Fort E Dive

9 x 6 = 54

Sign x Chicks = Fishing with Core

9 x 7 = 63

Sign x Surfin' = Sticky Bee

9 x 8 = 72

Sign x Skate = 72 MPH

9 x 9 = 81

Sign x Sign = Ate a Ton

4 x 7 = 28

**Door x Surfin' =
Denty Plate**

4 x 8 = 32

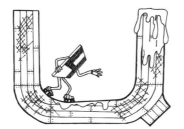

**Door x Skate =
Dirty U**

6 x 7 = 42

**Chicks x Surfin' =
Fort E Zoo**

6 x 8 = 48

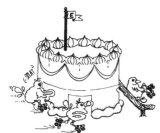

**Chicks x Skate =
Fort E Cake**

6 x 9 = 54

**Chicks x Sign =
Fishing with Core**

7 x 7 = 49

**Surfin' x Surfin' =
Fort E Twine**

7 x 8 = 56

**Surfin' x Skate =
Fishing for Sticks**

7 x 9 = 63

**Surfin' x Sign =
Sticky Bee**

8 x 9 = 72

**Skate x Sign =
72 MPH**

Using Flash Cards

One of the best ways for students to review the multiplication facts is to use flash cards. Both large and small flash card masters are included with <u>Multiplication in Minutes: The Times Tables</u>. Duplicate the flash card pages with the pictures on the front and the corresponding answer on the back.

Large Flash Cards

The large group flash cards are designed to be used with the entire class or in small groups. A successful way of using the large flash cards is to hold up a card with the front toward the class. The students stand, rather than raising their hand, when they know the correct answer. Call on individual students who are standing to give the answer. Having the students stand keeps them focused and forces them to be active participants rather than passive listeners.

Photocopies of the picture side of the flash cards also double as coloring pages. Many teachers have students make a booklet from the coloring pages as they progress through the multiplication facts.

Around the World:
Large group flash cards are great for *Around the World*. Students sit in a circle. Choose a starting person. This student stands behind the next student in the circle. The teacher holds up a flash card. The first student to say the answer stands behind the next person in the circle. If a sitting student says the answer first, the standing student sits down in the winner's chair. This process continues until at least one student makes it completely around the circle.

Around the World is also a good game for small groups of students who need some extra help on certain multiplication facts. Have a student be the group leader and coordinate a game of *Around the World* for that group.

Instead of having the students say the answer, another twist to the game is to have the students say the picture they remember. For example, if the multiplication fact is 3 x 4, the student should respond 'elf' rather than twelve.

Team Tag:
Divide the students into two groups. Have them form two single file lines facing forward. The first student should be about 10 feet from the front of the room. Put two equal stacks of flash cards on a desk in the front of the room.

When play starts, the first person in line races to the desk, takes the first card in his or her pile, holds it up, announces the answer to the class, places the card in a discard pile, and then races to tag the next person in line. If the student does not know the answer or gives the wrong answer, he or she puts the card on the bottom of the pile and selects the next card. This student keeps selecting cards until he or she knows the answer to one or until five cards have been selected.

The two teams play simultaneously. The first team to correctly give the answer to all the multiplication facts in their pile wins.

Small Student Flash Cards

Give students two sets of small flash cards. One set stays at school and the other set is to be kept at home. It is a good idea for each student to put his or her name or initials on each card. The cards can be kept in an envelope, rubber banded together, or a hole can be punched in each card so they can be kept on a ring. These storage methods will prevent loss.

At School Practice:
Students should be encouraged to study the multiplication facts using their small flash cards whenever they have free time. This activity can be reinforced by giving praise and encouragement to students who choose to practice.

Partner students who are having problems with certain multiplication facts with students who are not having trouble with them. That way, students who are having problems have a one-on-one tutor. One method of partnering students is to rank order a quiz you give over the facts. Put the number one ranked student with the student ranked last. Have the next ranked student work with the next-to-last student, and so on.

At Home Practice:
Students should study their flash cards each evening. The students may study the cards by themselves or with help from a parent or sibling.

One successful strategy is for students to study the flash cards while they watch TV. During each commercial, they go through the flash cards. Students make two piles of cards. One pile is made up of the multiplication facts they know. The other pile consists of the facts with which they are having problems. Students should keep going through the pile of problem facts.

3

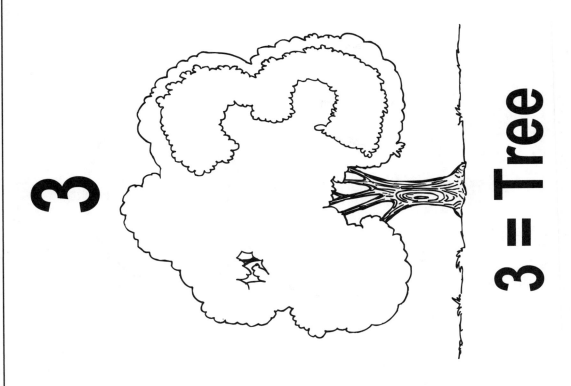

3 = Tree

Memorize in Minutes: The Times Tables
www.multplication.com

2

2 = Shoe

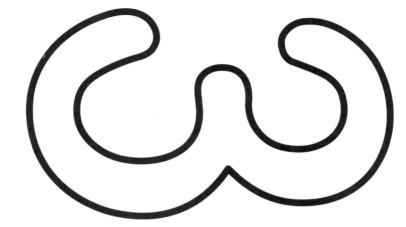

Memorize in Minutes: The Times Tables
www.multiplication.com

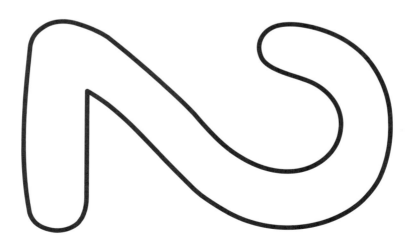

Memorize in Minutes: The Times Tables
www.multiplication.com

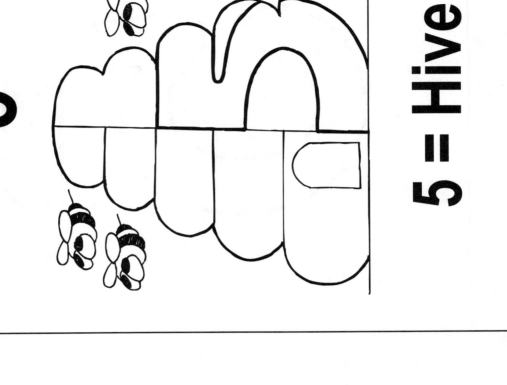

5

5 = Hive

4

4 = Door

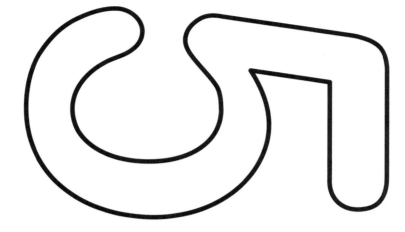

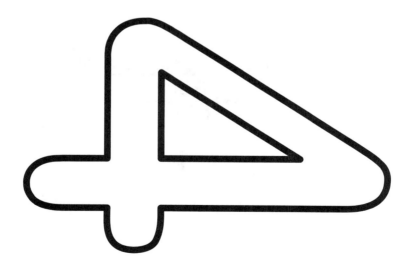

7

7 = Surfin'

6

6 = Chick

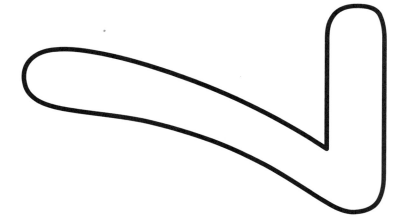

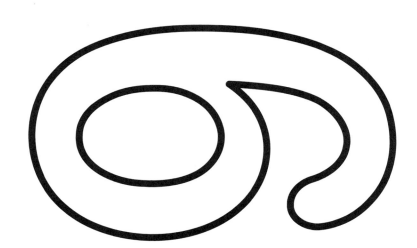

9

9 = Sign

8

8 = Skate

Memorize in Minutes: The Times Tables
www.multiplication.com

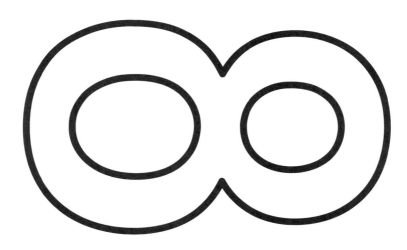

Memorize in Minutes: The Times Tables
www.multiplication.com

Coloring Page

2 x 3 = 6

Shoe x Tree =
Sticks

2 x 2 = 4

Shoe x Shoe =
Floor

Memorize in Minutes: The Times Tables
www.multiplication.com

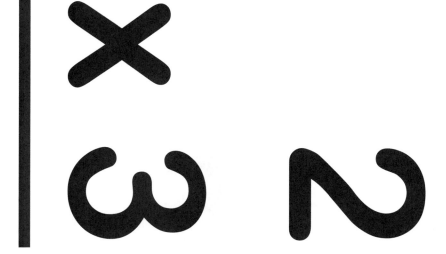

2
× 3

2
× 2

2 x 5 = 10

Shoe x Hive =
Pen

2 x 4 = 8

Shoe x Door =
Plate

Memorize in Minutes: The Times Tables
www.multiplication.com

$$2 \times 5$$

$$2 \times 4$$

2 x 7 = 14

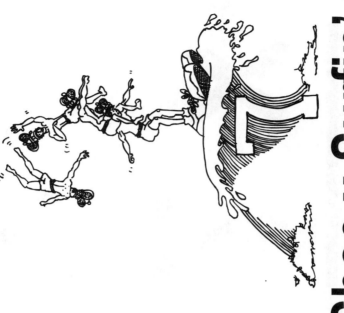

Shoe x Surfin' = Four Kings

2 x 6 = 12

Shoe x Chick = Elf

Memorize in Minutes: The Times Tables
www.multiplication.com

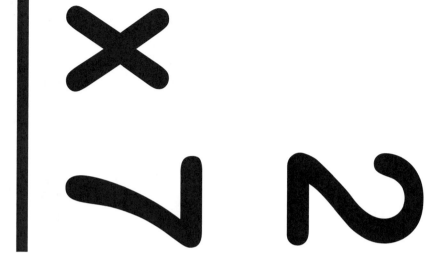

$$2 \times 7$$

$$2 \times 6$$

Memorize in Minutes: The Times Tables
www.multiplication.com

Memorize in Minutes: The Times Tables
www.multiplication.com

2 x 8 = 16

2 x 9 = 18

Shoe x Skate =
Sick Queen

Shoe x Sign =
Aching

2
x 6
___

2
x 8
___

3 x 4 = 12

Tree x Door =
Elf

3 x 3 = 9

Tree x Tree =
Line

3
× 4

3
× 3

Memorize in Minutes: The Times Tables
www.multiplication.com

Memorize in Minutes: The Times Tables
www.multiplication.com

3 x 6 = 18

Tree x Chicks = Aching

3 x 5 = 15

Tree x Hive = Lifting

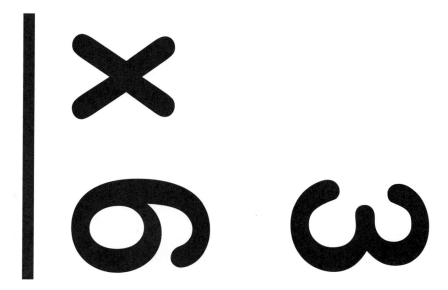

$$3 \times 6$$

$$3 \times 5$$

Memorize in Minutes: The Times Tables
www.multiplication.com

Memorize in Minutes: The Times Tables
www.multiplication.com

3 x 8 = 24

Tree x Skate = Denty Floor

3 x 7 = 21

Tree x Surfin' = Denty Sun

3
× 8

3
× 7

Memorize in Minutes: The Times Tables
www.multiplication.com

Memorize in Minutes: The Times Tables
www.multiplication.com

Coloring Page

4 x 4 = 16

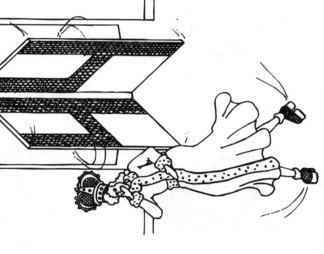

Door x Door =
Sick Queen

3 x 9 = 27

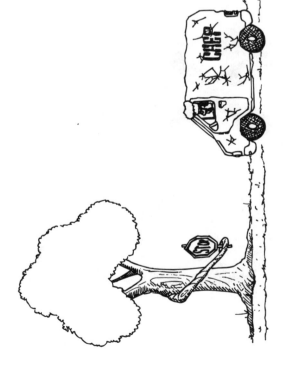

Tree x Sign =
Denty Chef's Van

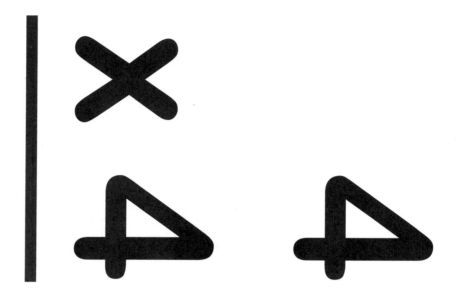

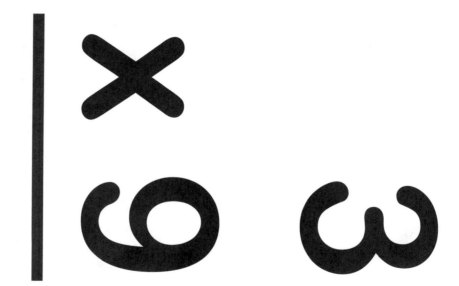

Memorize in Minutes: The Times Tables
www.multiplication.com

Memorize in Minutes: The Times Tables
www.multiplication.com

4 x 6 = 24

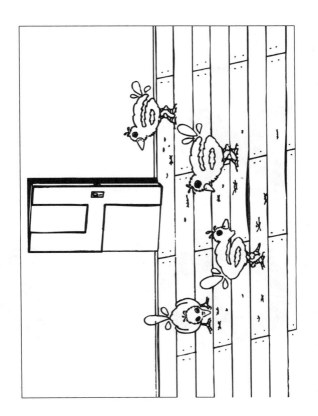

Door x Chicks = Denty Floor

4 x 5 = 20

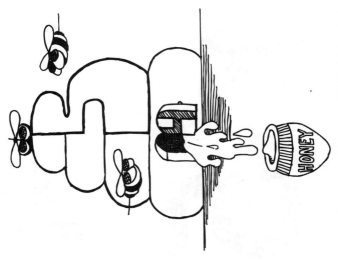

Door x Hive = Honey

Memorize in Minutes: The Times Tables
www.multiplication.com

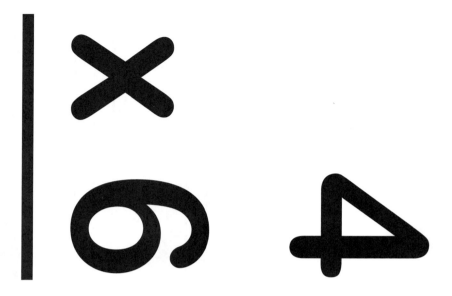

$$4 \times 6$$

$$4 \times 5$$

Memorize in Minutes: The Times Tables
www.multiplication.com

Memorize in Minutes: The Times Tables
www.multiplication.com

4 x 8 = 32

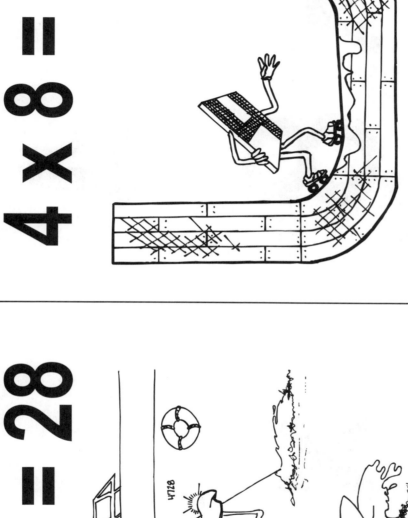

Door x Skate = Dirty U

4 x 7 = 28

Door x Surfin' = Denty Plate

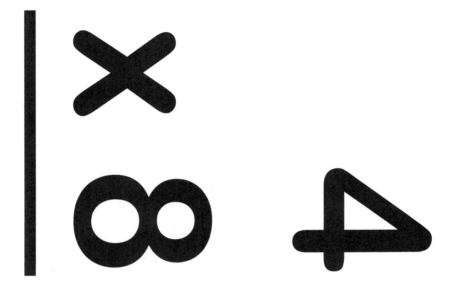

4 × 8

4 × 7

Coloring Page

5 x 5 = 25

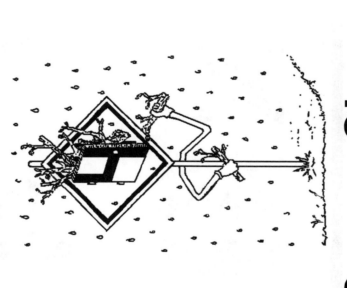

Hive x Hive = Denty Dive

4 x 9 = 36

Door x Sign = Dirty Sticks

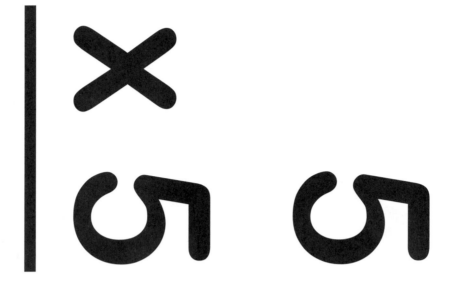

$$5 \times 5$$

$$4 \times 6$$

Memorize in Minutes: The Times Tables
www.multiplication.com

Memorize in Minutes: The Times Tables
www.multiplication.com

5 x 7 = 35

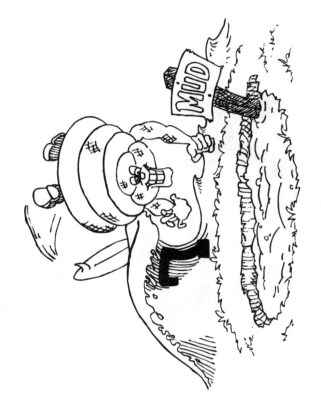

Hive x Surfin' = Dirty Dive

5 x 6 = 30

Hive x Chicks = Dirty

Memorize in Minutes: The Times Tables
www.multiplication.com

5

× 7

5

× 6

5 x 9 = 45

Hive x Sign =
Fort E Dive

5 x 8 = 40

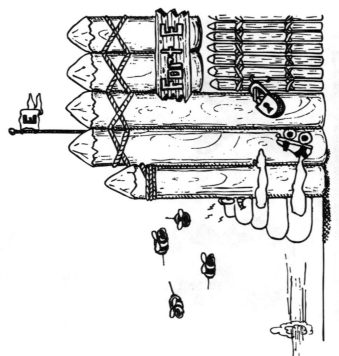

Hive x Skate =
Fort E

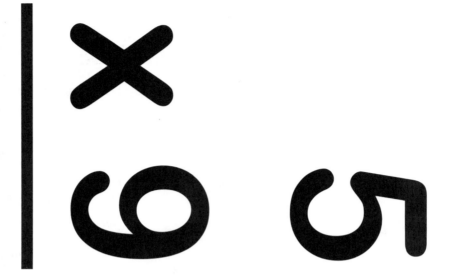

5
x 9

5
x 8

Coloring Page

6 x 7 = 42

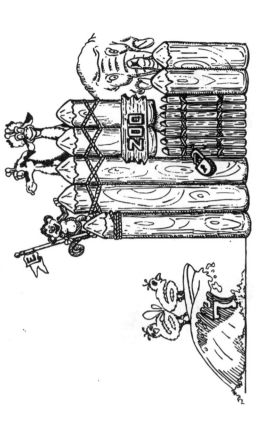

Chicks x Surfin' = Fort E Zoo

6 x 6 = 36

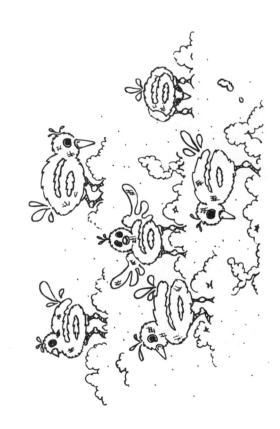

Chicks x Chicks = Dirty Chicks

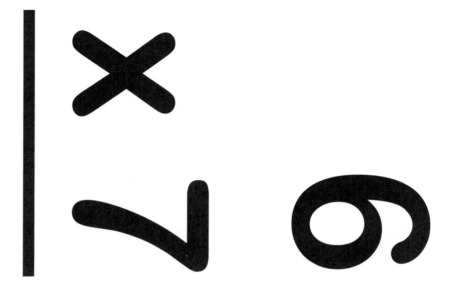

6 × 7

6 × 9

Memorize in Minutes: The Times Tables
www.multiplication.com

Memorize in Minutes: The Times Tables
www.multiplication.com

6 x 9 = 54

Chicks x Sign = Fishing with Core

6 x 8 = 48

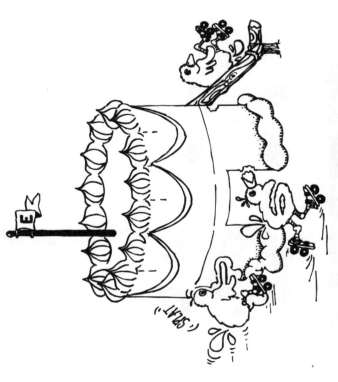

Chicks x Skates = Fort E Cake

Memorize in Minutes: The Times Tables
www.multiplication.com

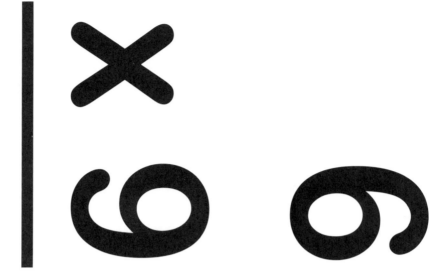

9
× 9

9
× 8

Memorize in Minutes: The Times Tables
www.multiplication.com

Memorize in Minutes: The Times Tables
www.multiplication.com

7 x 8 = 56

Surfin' x Skates =
Fishing for Sticks

7 x 7 = 49

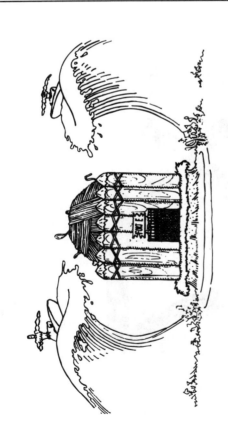

Surfin' x Surfin' =
Fort E Twine

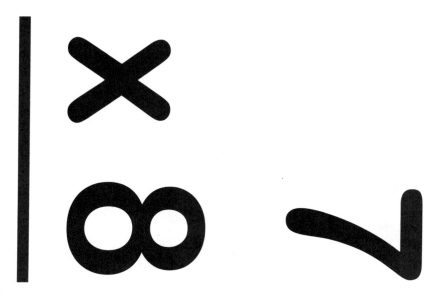

7 × 8

7 × 7

8 x 8 = 64

Skate x Skate = Sticky Floor

7 x 9 = 63

Surfin' x Sign = Sticky Bee

8 × 8

7 × 9

Memorize in Minutes: The Times Tables
www.multiplication.com

Memorize in Minutes: The Times Tables
www.multiplication.com

9 x 9 = 81

Sign x Sign =
Ate a Ton

8 x 9 = 72

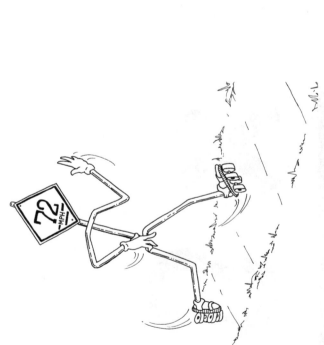

Skate x Sign =
72 MPH

Memorize in Minutes: The Times Tables
www.multiplication.com

9 × 9

9

9 × 9

8

Memorize in Minutes: The Times Tables
www.multiplication.com

Memorize in Minutes: The Times Tables
www.multiplication.com

2 x 2 = 4

**Shoe x Shoe =
Floor**

2 x 3 = 6

**Shoe x Tree =
Sticks**

2 x 4 = 8

**Shoe x Door =
Plate**

2 x 5 = 10

**Shoe x Hive =
Pen**

2 x 6 = 12

**Shoe x Chick =
Elf**

2 x 7 = 14

**Shoe x Surfin' =
Four Kings**

2 x 8 = 16

**Shoe x Skate =
Sick Queen**

2 x 9 = 18

**Shoe x Sign =
Aching**

3 x 3 = 9

**Tree x Tree =
Line**

$$\begin{array}{r} 2 \\ \times\,4 \\ \hline \end{array} \qquad \begin{array}{r} 2 \\ \times\,3 \\ \hline \end{array} \qquad \begin{array}{r} 2 \\ \times\,2 \\ \hline \end{array}$$

$$\begin{array}{r} 2 \\ \times\,7 \\ \hline \end{array} \qquad \begin{array}{r} 2 \\ \times\,6 \\ \hline \end{array} \qquad \begin{array}{r} 2 \\ \times\,5 \\ \hline \end{array}$$

$$\begin{array}{r} 3 \\ \times\,3 \\ \hline \end{array} \qquad \begin{array}{r} 2 \\ \times\,9 \\ \hline \end{array} \qquad \begin{array}{r} 2 \\ \times\,8 \\ \hline \end{array}$$

3 x 4 = 12

Tree x Door = Elf

3 x 5 = 15

Tree x Hive = Lifting

3 x 6 = 18

Tree x Chicks = Aching

3 x 7 = 21

Tree x Surfin' = Denty Sun

3 x 8 = 24

Tree x Skate = Denty Floor

3 x 9 = 27

Tree x Sign = Denty Chef's Van

4 x 4 = 16

Door x Door = Sick Queen

4 x 5 = 20

Door x Hive = Honey

4 x 6 = 24

Door x Chicks = Denty Floor

$$\begin{array}{r} 3 \\ \times\, 6 \\ \hline \end{array} \qquad \begin{array}{r} 3 \\ \times\, 5 \\ \hline \end{array} \qquad \begin{array}{r} 3 \\ \times\, 4 \\ \hline \end{array}$$

$$\begin{array}{r} 3 \\ \times\, 9 \\ \hline \end{array} \qquad \begin{array}{r} 3 \\ \times\, 8 \\ \hline \end{array} \qquad \begin{array}{r} 3 \\ \times\, 7 \\ \hline \end{array}$$

$$\begin{array}{r} 4 \\ \times\, 6 \\ \hline \end{array} \qquad \begin{array}{r} 4 \\ \times\, 5 \\ \hline \end{array} \qquad \begin{array}{r} 4 \\ \times\, 4 \\ \hline \end{array}$$

4 x 7 = 28

Door x Surfin' = Denty Plate

4 x 8 = 32

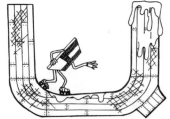

Door x Skates = Dirty U

4 x 9 = 36

Door x Sign = Dirty Sticks

5 x 5 = 25

Hive x Hive = Denty Dive

5 x 6 = 30

Hive x Chicks = Dirty

5 x 7 = 35

Hive x Surfin' = Dirty Dive

5 x 8 = 40

Hive x Skates = Fort E

5 x 9 = 45

Hive x Sign = Fort E Dive

6 x 6 = 36

Chicks x Chicks = Dirty Chicks

$$4 \times 9 \qquad 4 \times 8 \qquad 4 \times 7$$

$$5 \times 7 \qquad 5 \times 6 \qquad 5 \times 5$$

$$6 \times 6 \qquad 5 \times 9 \qquad 5 \times 8$$

6 x 7 = 42

**Chicks x Surfin' =
Fort E Zoo**

6 x 8 = 48

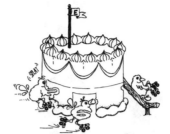

**Chicks x Skate =
Fort E Cake**

6 x 9 = 54

**Chicks x Sign =
Fishing with Core**

7 x 7 = 49

**Surfin' x Surfin' =
Fort E Twine**

7 x 8 = 56

**Surfin' x Skate =
Fishing for Sticks**

7 x 9 = 63

**Surfin' x Sign =
Sticky Bee**

8 x 8 = 64

**Skate x Skate =
Sticky Floor**

8 x 9 = 72

**Skate x Sign =
72 MPH**

9 x 9 = 81

**Sign x Sign =
Ate a Ton**

$$\begin{array}{r} 6 \\ \times\ 9 \\ \hline \end{array}$$

$$\begin{array}{r} 6 \\ \times\ 8 \\ \hline \end{array}$$

$$\begin{array}{r} 6 \\ \times\ 7 \\ \hline \end{array}$$

$$\begin{array}{r} 7 \\ \times\ 9 \\ \hline \end{array}$$

$$\begin{array}{r} 7 \\ \times\ 8 \\ \hline \end{array}$$

$$\begin{array}{r} 7 \\ \times\ 7 \\ \hline \end{array}$$

$$\begin{array}{r} 9 \\ \times\ 9 \\ \hline \end{array}$$

$$\begin{array}{r} 8 \\ \times\ 9 \\ \hline \end{array}$$

$$\begin{array}{r} 8 \\ \times\ 8 \\ \hline \end{array}$$

Student Record Chart

Date _____

Chart 1 2 x 2 - 4 x 6 (Student Names)	2 x2	2 x3	2 x4	2 x5	2 x6	2 x7	2 x8	2 x9	3 x3	3 x4	3 x5	3 x6	3 x7	3 x8	3 x9	4 x4	4 x5	4 x6

Student Record Chart

Date _____

Chart 2 4 x 7 - 9 x 9 (Student Names)	4 x7	4 x8	4 x9	5 x5	5 x6	5 x7	5 x8	5 x9	6 x6	6 x7	6 x8	6 x9	7 x7	7 x8	7 x9	8 x8	8 x9	9 x9

Memorize in Minutes: The Times Tables
www.multiplication.com

Order Form

Fax Orders:

Fax orders to: **(509) 786-7978**

World Wide Web Orders:

Visit our web site at: **http//www.multiplication.com**

Postal Orders:

Mail your order to: **Krimsten Publishing, P.O. Box 48, Prosser, WA 99350, USA**

Name:_____

School:_____

Address:_____

City:_____ State:_____ Zip:_____

Telephone: (_____) _____

Quantity	Publication	Price	Sub-total
_____	**Memorize in Minutes, The Times Tables** *Teacher Manual*	**$29.95**	_____
	Please add sales tax for books shipped to Washington addresses		_____
		Subtotal	_____
		Shipping	_$ 4.50_
		Total	_____

Payment:

☐ Check ☐ VISA ☐ Mastercard

☐ School Purchase Order# _____ (Call for quantity discount)

Card Number:_____

Name on Card:_____ Exp. Date_____

Prices subject to change without notice.

Visit our web site for other publications and products.

Order Form

Fax Orders:

Fax orders to: **(509) 786-7978**

World Wide Web Orders:

Visit our web site at: **http//www.multiplication.com**

Postal Orders:

Mail your order to: **Krimsten Publishing, P.O. Box 48, Prosser, WA 99350, USA**

Name:_____

School:_____

Address:_____

City:_____ State:_____ Zip:_____

Telephone: (_____) _____

Quantity	Publication	Price	Sub-total
_____	**Memorize in Minutes, The Times Tables** *Teacher Manual*	$29.95	_____
	Please add sales tax for books shipped to Washington addresses		_____
		Subtotal	_____
		Shipping	**$ 4.50**
		Total	_____

Payment:

☐ Check ☐ VISA ☐ Mastercard

☐ School Purchase Order# _____ (Call for quantity discount)

Card Number:_____

Name on Card:_____ Exp. Date_____

Prices subject to change without notice.

Visit our web site for other publications and products.